GREAT PREACHERS

The Pursuit of God
by
A. W. Tozer

Lord, Teach us to Pray
by
Andrew Murray

All of Grace
by
Charles H. Spurgeon

Sinners in the Hands of an Angry God
by
Jonathan Edwards

Contents

The Pursuit of God
by A. W. Tozer · · · · · · · · · · · · · · · · · · · 7

Lord, Teach us to Pray
by Andrew Murray · · · · · · · · · · · · · · · · · 81

All of Grace
by Charles Spurgeon · · · · · · · · · · · · · · · · 103

Sinners in the hands of an angry God
by Jonathan Edwards · · · · · · · · · · · · · · · · 191

The Pursuit of God

by

A. W. Tozer

*"Then shall we know,
if we follow on to know the Lord:
his going forth is prepared as the morning."*
hosea 6:3

Preface

In this hour of all-but-universal darkness one cheering gleam appears: within the fold of conservative Christianity there are to be found increasing numbers of persons whose religious lives are marked by a growing hunger after God Himself. They are eager for spiritual realities and will not be put off with words, nor will they be content with correct "interpretations" of truth. They are athirst for God, and they will not be satisfied till they have drunk deep at the Fountain of Living Water.

This is the only real harbinger of revival which I have been able to detect anywhere on the religious horizon. It may be the cloud the size of a man's hand for which a few saints here and there have been looking. It can result in a resurrection of life for many souls and a recapture of that radiant wonder which should accompany faith in Christ, that wonder which has all but fled the Church of God in our day.

But this hunger must be recognized by our religious leaders. Current evangelicalism has (to change the figure) laid the altar and divided the sacrifice into parts, but now seems satisfied to count the stones and rearrange the pieces with never a care that there is not a sign of fire upon the top of lofty Carmel. But God be thanked that there are a few who care. They are those who, while they love the altar and delight in the sacrifice, are yet unable to reconcile themselves to the continued absence of fire. They desire God above all. They are athirst to taste for themselves the "piercing sweetness" of the love of Christ about Whom all the holy prophets did write and the psalmists did sing.

There is today no lack of Bible teachers to set forth correctly the principles of the doctrines of Christ, but too many of these seem satisfied to teach the fundamentals of the faith year after year, strangely unaware that there is in their ministry no manifest Presence, nor anything unusual in their personal lives. They minister constantly to believers who feel within their breasts a longing which their teaching simply does not satisfy.

I trust I speak in charity, but the lack in our pulpits is real. Milton's terrible sentence applies to our day as accurately as it did to his: "The hungry sheep look up, and are not fed." It is a solemn thing, and no small scandal in the Kingdom, to see God's children starving while actually seated at the Father's table. The truth of Wesley's words is established before our eyes: "Orthodoxy, or right opinion, is, at best, a very slender part of religion. Though right tempers cannot subsist without right opinions, yet right opinions may subsist without right tempers. There may be a right opinion of God without either love or one right temper toward Him. Satan is a proof of this."

Thanks to our splendid Bible societies and to other effective agencies for the dissemination of the Word, there are today many millions of people who hold "right opinions," probably more than ever before in the history of the Church. Yet I wonder if there was ever a time when true spiritual worship was at a lower ebb. To great sections of the Church the art of worship has been lost entirely, and in its place has come that strange and foreign thing called the "program." This word has been borrowed from the stage and applied with sad wisdom to the type of public service which now passes for worship among us.

Sound Bible exposition is an imperative *must* in the Church of the Living God. Without it no church can be a New Testament church in any strict meaning of that term. But exposition may be carried on in such way as to leave the hearers devoid of any true spiritual nourishment whatever. For it is not mere words that nourish the soul, but God Himself, and unless and until the hearers find God in personal experience they are not the better for having heard the truth. The Bible is not an end in itself, but a means to bring men to an intimate and satisfying knowledge of God, that they may enter into Him, that they may delight in His Presence, may taste and know the inner sweetness of the very God Himself in the core and center of their hearts.

This book is a modest attempt to aid God's hungry children so to find Him. Nothing here is new except in the sense that it is a discovery which my own heart has made of spiritual realities most delightful and wonderful to me. Others before me have gone much farther into these holy mysteries than I have done, but if my fire is not large it is yet real, and there may be those who can light their candle at its flame.

    A. W. Tozer

I *Following Hard after God*

> My soul followeth hard after thee: thy right hand upholdeth me.—*Psa. 63:8*

Christian theology teaches the doctrine of prevenient grace, which briefly stated means this, that before a man can seek God, God must first have sought the man.

Before a sinful man can think a right thought of God, there must have been a work of enlightenment done within him; imperfect it may be, but a true work nonetheless, and the secret cause of all desiring and seeking and praying which may follow.

We pursue God because, and only because, He has first put an urge within us that spurs us to the pursuit. "No man can come to me," said our Lord, "except the Father which hath sent me draw him," and it is by this very prevenient *drawing* that God takes from us every vestige of credit for the act of coming. The impulse to pursue God originates with God, but the outworking of that impulse is our following hard after Him; and all the time we are pursuing Him we are already in His hand: "Thy right hand upholdeth me."

In this divine "upholding" and human "following" there is no contradiction. All is of God, for as von Hügel teaches, *God is always previous*. In practice, however, (that is, where God's previous working meets man's present response) man must pursue God. On our part there must be positive reciprocation if this secret drawing of God is to eventuate in identifiable experience of the Divine. In the warm language of personal feeling this is stated in the Forty-second Psalm: "As the hart panteth after the water brooks, so panteth my soul after thee, O God. My soul thirsteth for God, for the living God: when shall I come and appear before God?" This is deep calling unto deep, and the longing heart will understand it.

The doctrine of justification by faith—a Biblical truth, and a blessed relief from sterile legalism and unavailing self-effort—has in our time fallen into evil company and been interpreted by many in such manner as actually to bar men from the knowledge of God. The whole transaction of religious conversion has been made mechanical and spiritless. Faith may now be exercised without a jar to the moral life and without embarrassment to the Adamic ego. Christ may be "received" without creating any special love for Him in the soul of the receiver. The man is "saved," but he is not hungry nor thirsty after God. In fact he is specifically taught to be satisfied and encouraged to be content with little.

The modern scientist has lost God amid the wonders of His world; we Christians are in real danger of losing God amid the wonders of His Word. We have almost forgotten that God is a Person and, as such, can be cultivated as any person can. It is inherent in personality to be able to know other personalities, but full knowledge of one personality by another cannot be achieved in one encounter. It is only after long and loving mental intercourse that the full possibilities of both can be explored.

All social intercourse between human beings is a response of personality to personality, grading upward from the most casual brush between man and man to the fullest, most intimate communion of which the human soul is capable. Religion, so far as it is genuine, is in essence the response of created personalities to the Creating Personality, God. "This is life eternal, that they might know thee the only true God, and Jesus Christ, whom thou hast sent."

God is a Person, and in the deep of His mighty nature He thinks, wills, enjoys, feels, loves, desires and suffers as any other person may. In making Himself known to us He stays by the familiar pattern of personality. He communicates with us through the avenues of our minds, our wills and our emotions. The continuous and unembarrassed interchange of love and thought between God and the soul of the redeemed man is the throbbing heart of New Testament religion.

This intercourse between God and the soul is known to us in conscious personal awareness. It is personal: that is, it does not come through the body of believers, as such, but is known to the individual, and to the body through the individuals which compose it. And it is conscious: that is, it does not stay below the threshold of consciousness and work there unknown to the soul (as, for instance, infant baptism is thought by some to do), but comes within the field of awareness where the man can "know" it as he knows any other fact of experience.

You and I are in little (our sins excepted) what God is in large. Being made in His image we have within us the capacity to know Him. In our sins we lack only the power. The moment the Spirit has quickened us to life in regeneration our whole being senses its kinship to God and leaps up in joyous recognition. That is the heavenly birth without which we cannot see the Kingdom of God. It is, however, not an end but an inception, for now begins the glorious pursuit, the heart's happy exploration of the infinite riches of the Godhead. That is where we begin, I say, but where we stop no man has yet discovered, for there is in the awful and mysterious depths of the Triune God neither limit nor end.

Shoreless Ocean, who can sound Thee? Thine own eternity is round Thee, Majesty divine!

To have found God and still to pursue Him is the soul's paradox of love, scorned indeed by the too-easily-satisfied religionist, but justified in happy experience by the children of the burning heart. St. Bernard stated this holy paradox in a musical quatrain that will be instantly understood by every worshipping soul:

We taste Thee, O Thou Living Bread, And long to feast upon Thee still: We drink of Thee, the Fountainhead And thirst our souls from Thee to fill.

Come near to the holy men and women of the past and you will soon feel the heat of their desire after God. They mourned for Him, they prayed and wrestled and sought for Him day and night, in season and out, and when they had found Him the finding was all the sweeter for the long seeking. Moses used the fact that he knew God as an argument for knowing Him better. "Now, therefore, I pray thee, if I have found grace in thy sight, show me now thy way, that I may know thee, that I may find grace in thy sight"; and from there he rose to make the daring request, "I beseech thee, show me thy glory." God was frankly pleased by this display of ardor, and the next day called Moses into the mount, and there in solemn procession made all His glory pass before him.

David's life was a torrent of spiritual desire, and his psalms ring with the cry of the seeker and the glad shout of the finder. Paul confessed the mainspring of his life to be his burning desire after Christ. "That I may know Him," was the goal of his heart, and to this he sacrificed everything. "Yea doubtless, and I count all things but loss for the excellency of the knowledge of Christ Jesus my Lord: for whom I have suffered the loss of all things, and do count them but refuse, that I may win Christ."

Hymnody is sweet with the longing after God, the God whom, while the singer seeks, he knows he has already found. "His track I see and I'll pursue," sang our fathers only a short generation ago, but that song is heard no more in the great congregation. How tragic that we in this dark day have had our seeking done for us by our teachers. Everything is made to center upon the initial act of "accepting" Christ (a term, incidentally, which is not found in the Bible) and we are not expected thereafter to crave any further revelation of God to our souls. We have been snared in the coils of a spurious logic which insists that if we have found Him we need no more seek Him. This is set before us as the last word in orthodoxy, and it is taken for granted that no Bible-taught Christian ever believed otherwise. Thus the whole testimony of the worshipping, seeking, singing Church on that subject is crisply set aside. The experiential heart-theology of a grand army of fragrant saints is rejected in favor of a smug interpretation of Scripture which would certainly have sounded strange to an Augustine, a Rutherford or a Brainerd.

In the midst of this great chill there are some, I rejoice to acknowledge, who will not be content with shallow logic. They will admit the force of the argument, and then turn away with tears to hunt some lonely place and pray, "O God, show me thy glory." They want to taste, to touch with their hearts, to see with their inner eyes the wonder that is God.

I want deliberately to encourage this mighty longing after God. The lack of it has brought us to our present low estate. The stiff and wooden quality about our religious lives is a result of our lack of holy desire. Complacency is a deadly foe of all spiritual growth. Acute desire must be present or there will be no manifestation of Christ to His people. He waits to be wanted. Too bad that with many of us He waits so long, so very long, in vain.

Every age has its own characteristics. Right now we are in an age of religious complexity. The simplicity which is in Christ is rarely found among us. In its stead are programs, methods, organizations and a world of nervous activities which occupy time and attention but can never satisfy the longing of the heart. The shallowness of our inner experience, the hollowness of our worship, and that servile imitation of the world which marks our promotional methods all testify that we, in this day, know God only imperfectly, and the peace of God scarcely at all.

If we would find God amid all the religious externals we must first determine to find Him, and then proceed in the way of simplicity. Now as always God discovers Himself to "babes" and hides Himself in thick darkness from the wise and the prudent. We must simplify our approach to Him. We must strip down to essentials (and they will be found to be blessedly few). We must put away all effort to impress, and come with the guileless candor of childhood. If we do this, without doubt God will quickly respond.

When religion has said its last word, there is little that we need other than God Himself. The evil habit of seeking *God-and* effectively prevents us from finding God in full revelation. In the "and" lies our great woe. If we omit the "and" we shall soon find God, and in Him we shall find that for which we have all our lives been secretly longing.

We need not fear that in seeking God only we may narrow our lives or restrict the motions of our expanding hearts. The opposite is true. We can well afford to make God our All, to concentrate, to sacrifice the many for the One.

The author of the quaint old English classic, *The Cloud of Unknowing*, teaches us how to do this. "Lift up thine heart unto God with a meek stirring of love; and mean Himself, and none of His goods. And thereto, look thee loath to think on aught but God Himself. So that nought work in thy wit, nor in thy will, but only God Himself. This is the work of the soul that most pleaseth God."

Again, he recommends that in prayer we practice a further stripping down of everything, even of our theology. "For it sufficeth enough, a naked intent direct unto God without any other cause than Himself." Yet underneath all his thinking lay the broad foundation of New Testament truth, for he explains that by "Himself" he means "God that made thee, and bought thee, and that graciously called thee to thy degree." And he is all for simplicity: If we would have religion "lapped and folden in one word, for that thou shouldst have better hold thereupon, take thee but a little word of one syllable: for so it is better than of two, for even the shorter it is the better it accordeth with the work of the Spirit. And such a word is this word GOD or this word LOVE."

When the Lord divided Canaan among the tribes of Israel Levi received no share of the land. God said to him simply, "I am thy part and thine inheritance," and by those words made him richer than all his brethren, richer than all the kings and rajas who have ever lived in the world. And there is a spiritual principle here, a principle still valid for every priest of the Most High God.

The man who has God for his treasure has all things in One. Many ordinary treasures may be denied him, or if he is allowed to have them, the enjoyment of them will be so tempered that they will never be necessary to his happiness. Or if he must see them go, one after one, he will scarcely feel a sense of loss, for having the Source of all things he has in One all satisfaction, all pleasure, all delight. Whatever he may lose he has actually lost nothing, for he now has it all in One, and he has it purely, legitimately and forever.

O God, I have tasted Thy goodness, and it has both satisfied me and made me thirsty for more. I am painfully conscious of my need of further grace. I am ashamed of my lack of desire. O God, the Triune God, I want to want Thee; I long to be filled with longing; I thirst to be made more thirsty still. Show me Thy glory, I pray Thee, that so I may know Thee indeed. Begin in mercy a new work of love within me. Say to my soul, "Rise up, my love, my fair one, and come away." Then give me grace to rise and follow Thee up from this misty lowland where I have wandered so long. In Jesus' Name, Amen.

II *The Blessedness of Possessing Nothing*

> Blessed are the poor in spirit: for theirs is the kingdom of heaven.—*Matt. 5:3*

Before the Lord God made man upon the earth He first prepared for him by creating a world of useful and pleasant things for his sustenance and delight. In the Genesis account of the creation these are called simply "things." They were made for man's uses, but they were meant always to be external to the man and subservient to him. In the deep heart of the man was a shrine where none but God was worthy to come. Within him was God; without, a thousand gifts which God had showered upon him.

But sin has introduced complications and has made those very gifts of God a potential source of ruin to the soul.

Our woes began when God was forced out of His central shrine and "things" were allowed to enter. Within the human heart "things" have taken over. Men have now by nature no peace within their hearts, for God is crowned there no longer, but there in the moral dusk stubborn and aggressive usurpers fight among themselves for first place on the throne.

This is not a mere metaphor, but an accurate analysis of our real spiritual trouble. There is within the human heart a tough fibrous root of fallen life whose nature is to possess, always to possess. It covets "things" with a deep and fierce passion. The pronouns "my" and "mine" look innocent enough in print, but their constant and universal use is significant. They express the real nature of the old Adamic man better than a thousand volumes of theology could do. They are verbal symptoms of our deep disease. The roots of our hearts have grown down into *things*, and we dare not pull up one rootlet lest we die. Things have become necessary to us, a development never originally intended. God's gifts now take the place of God, and the whole course of nature is upset by the monstrous substitution.

Our Lord referred to this tyranny of *things* when He said to His disciples, "If any man will come after me, let him deny himself, and take up his cross, and follow me. For whosoever will save his life shall lose it: and whosoever shall lose his life for my sake shall find it."

Breaking this truth into fragments for our better understanding, it would seem that there is within each of us an enemy which we tolerate at our peril. Jesus called it "life" and "self," or as we would say, the *self-life*. Its chief characteristic is its possessiveness: the words "gain" and "profit" suggest this. To allow this enemy to live is in the end to lose everything. To repudiate it and give up all for Christ's sake is to lose nothing at last, but to preserve everything unto life eternal. And possibly also a hint is given here as to the only effective way to destroy this foe: it is by the Cross. "Let him take up his cross and follow me."

The way to deeper knowledge of God is through the lonely valleys of soul poverty and abnegation of all things. The blessed ones who possess the Kingdom are they who have repudiated every external thing and have rooted from their hearts all sense of possessing. These are the "poor in spirit." They have reached an inward state paralleling the outward circumstances of the common beggar in the streets of Jerusalem; that is what the word "poor" as Christ used it actually means. These blessed poor are no longer slaves to the tyranny of *things*. They have broken the yoke of the oppressor; and this they have done not by fighting but by surrendering. Though free from all sense of possessing, they yet possess all things. "Theirs is the kingdom of heaven."

Let me exhort you to take this seriously. It is not to be understood as mere Bible teaching to be stored away in the mind along with an inert mass of other doctrines. It is a marker on the road to greener pastures, a path chiseled against the steep sides of the mount of God. We dare not try to by-pass it if we would follow on in this holy pursuit. We must ascend a step at a time. If we refuse one step we bring our progress to an end.

As is frequently true, this New Testament principle of spiritual life finds its best illustration in the Old Testament. In the story of Abraham and Isaac we have a dramatic picture of the surrendered life as well as an excellent commentary on the first Beatitude.

Abraham was old when Isaac was born, old enough indeed to have been his grandfather, and the child became at once the delight and idol of his heart. From that moment when he first stooped to take the tiny form awkwardly in his arms he was an eager love slave of his son. God went out of His way to comment on the strength of this affection. And it is not hard to understand. The baby represented everything sacred to his father's heart: the promises of God, the covenants, the hopes of the years and the long messianic dream. As he watched him grow from babyhood to young manhood the heart of the old man was knit closer and closer with the life of his son, till at last the relationship bordered upon the perilous. It was then that God stepped in to save both father and son from the consequences of an uncleansed love.

"Take now thy son," said God to Abraham, "thine only son Isaac, whom thou lovest, and get thee into the land of Moriah; and offer him there for a burnt-offering upon one of the mountains which I will tell thee of." The sacred writer spares us a close-up of the agony that night on the slopes near Beersheba when the aged man had it out with his God, but respectful imagination may view in awe the bent form and convulsive wrestling alone under the stars. Possibly not again until a Greater than Abraham wrestled in the Garden of Gethsemane did such mortal pain visit a human soul. If only the man himself might have been allowed to die. That would have been easier a thousand times, for he was old now, and to die would have been no great ordeal for one who had walked so long with God. Besides, it would have been a last sweet pleasure to let his dimming vision rest upon the figure of his stalwart son who would live to carry on the Abrahamic line and fulfill in himself the promises of God made long before in Ur of the Chaldees.

How should he slay the lad! Even if he could get the consent of his wounded and protesting heart, how could he reconcile the act with the promise, "In Isaac shall thy seed be called"? This was Abraham's trial by fire, and he did not fail in the crucible. While the stars still shone like sharp white points above the tent where the sleeping Isaac lay, and long before the gray dawn had begun to lighten the east, the old saint had made up his mind. He would offer his son as God had directed him to do, and *then trust God to raise him from the dead*. This, says the writer to the Hebrews, was the solution his aching heart found sometime in the dark night, and he rose "early in the morning" to carry out the plan. It is beautiful to see that, while he erred as to God's method, he had correctly sensed the secret of His great heart. And the solution accords well with the New Testament Scripture, "Whosoever will lose for my sake shall find."

God let the suffering old man go through with it up to the point where He knew there would be no retreat, and then forbade him to lay a hand upon the boy. To the wondering patriarch He now says in effect, "It's all right, Abraham. I never intended that you should actually slay the lad. I only wanted to remove him from the temple of your heart that I might reign unchallenged there. I wanted to correct the perversion that existed in your love. Now you may have the boy, sound and well. Take him and go back to your tent. Now I know that thou fearest God, seeing that thou hast not withheld thy son, thine only son, from me."

Then heaven opened and a voice was heard saying to him, "By myself have I sworn, saith the Lord, for because thou hast done this thing, and hast not withheld thy son, thine only son: that in blessing I will bless thee, and in multiplying I will multiply thy seed as the stars of the heaven, and as the sand which is upon the sea shore; and thy seed shall possess the gate of his enemies; and in thy seed shall all the nations of the earth be blessed; because thou hast obeyed my voice."

The old man of God lifted his head to respond to the Voice, and stood there on the mount strong and pure and grand, a man marked out by the Lord for special treatment, a friend and favorite of the Most High. Now he was a man wholly surrendered, a man utterly obedient, a man who possessed nothing. He had concentrated his all in the person of his dear son, and God had taken it from him. God could have begun out on the margin of Abraham's life and worked inward to the center; He chose rather to cut quickly to the heart and have it over in one sharp act of separation. In dealing thus He practiced an economy of means and time. It hurt cruelly, but it was effective.

I have said that Abraham possessed nothing. Yet was not this poor man rich? Everything he had owned before was his still to enjoy: sheep, camels, herds, and goods of every sort. He had also his wife and his friends, and best of all he had his son Isaac safe by his side. He had everything, but *he possessed nothing.* There is the spiritual secret. There is the sweet theology of the heart which can be learned only in the school of renunciation. The books on systematic theology overlook this, but the wise will understand.

After that bitter and blessed experience I think the words "my" and "mine" never had again the same meaning for Abraham. The sense of possession which they connote was gone from his heart. *Things* had been cast out forever. They had now become external to the man. His inner heart was free from them. The world said, "Abraham is rich," but the aged patriarch only smiled. He could not explain it to them, but he knew that he owned nothing, that his real treasures were inward and eternal.

There can be no doubt that this possessive clinging to things is one of the most harmful habits in the life. Because it is so natural it is rarely recognized for the evil that it is; but its outworkings are tragic.

We are often hindered from giving up our treasures to the Lord out of fear for their safety; this is especially true when those treasures are loved relatives and friends. But we need have no such fears. Our Lord came not to destroy but to save. Everything is safe which we commit to Him, and nothing is really safe which is not so committed.

Our gifts and talents should also be turned over to Him. They should be recognized for what they are, God's loan to us, and should never be considered in any sense our own. We have no more right to claim credit for special abilities than for blue eyes or strong muscles. "For who maketh thee to differ from another? and what hast thou that thou didst not receive?"

The Christian who is alive enough to know himself even slightly will recognize the symptoms of this possession malady, and will grieve to find them in his own heart. If the longing after God is strong enough within him he will want to do something about the matter. Now, what should he do?

First of all he should put away all defense and make no attempt to excuse himself either in his own eyes or before the Lord. Whoever defends himself will have himself for his defense, and he will have no other; but let him come defenseless before the Lord and he will have for his defender no less than God Himself. Let the inquiring Christian trample under foot every slippery trick of his deceitful heart and insist upon frank and open relations with the Lord.

Then he should remember that this is holy business. No careless or casual dealings will suffice. Let him come to God in full determination to be heard. Let him insist that God accept his all, that He take *things* out of his heart and Himself reign there in power. It may be he will need to become specific, to name things and people by their names one by one. If he will become drastic enough he can shorten the time of his travail from years to minutes and enter the good land long before his slower brethren who coddle their feelings and insist upon caution in their dealings with God.

Let us never forget that such a truth as this cannot be learned by rote as one would learn the facts of physical science. They must be *experienced* before we can really know them. We must in our hearts live through Abraham's harsh and bitter experiences if we would know the blessedness which follows them. The ancient curse will not go out painlessly; the tough old miser within us will not lie down and die obedient to our command. He must be torn out of our heart like a plant from the soil; he must be extracted in agony and blood like a tooth from the jaw. He must be expelled from our soul by violence as Christ expelled the money changers from the temple. And we shall need to steel ourselves against his piteous begging, and to recognize it as springing out of self-pity, one of the most reprehensible sins of the human heart.

If we would indeed know God in growing intimacy we must go this way of renunciation. And if we are set upon the pursuit of God He will sooner or later bring us to this test. Abraham's testing was, at the time, not known to him as such, yet if he had taken some course other than the one he did, the whole history of the Old Testament would have been different. God would have found His man, no doubt, but the loss to Abraham would have been tragic beyond the telling. So we will be brought one by one to the testing place, and we may never know when we are there. At that testing place there will be no dozen possible choices for us; just one and an alternative, but our whole future will be conditioned by the choice we make.

Father, I want to know Thee, but my coward heart fears to give up its toys. I cannot part with them without inward bleeding, and I do not try to hide from Thee the terror of the parting. I come trembling, but I do come. Please root from my heart all those things which I have cherished so long and which have become a very part of my living self, so that Thou mayest enter and dwell there without a rival. Then shalt Thou make the place of Thy feet glorious. Then shall my heart have no need of the sun to shine in it, for Thyself wilt be the light of it, and there shall be no night there. In Jesus' Name, Amen.

III *Removing the Veil*

> Having therefore, brethren, boldness to enter into the holiest by the blood of Jesus.—*Heb. 10:19*

Among the famous sayings of the Church fathers none is better known than Augustine's, "Thou hast formed us for Thyself, and our hearts are restless till they find rest in Thee."

The great saint states here in few words the origin and interior history of the human race. God made us for Himself: that is the only explanation that satisfies the *heart* of a thinking man, whatever his wild reason may say. Should faulty education and perverse reasoning lead a man to conclude otherwise, there is little that any Christian can do for him. For such a man I have no message. My appeal is addressed to those who have been previously taught in secret by the wisdom of God; I speak to thirsty hearts whose longings have been wakened by the touch of God within them, and such as they need no reasoned proof. Their restless hearts furnish all the proof they need.

God formed us for Himself. The *Shorter Catechism*, "Agreed upon by the Reverend Assembly of Divines at Westminster," as the old *New-England Primer* has it, asks the ancient questions *what* and *why* and answers them in one short sentence hardly matched in any uninspired work. "*Question*: What is the chief End of Man? *Answer*: Man's chief End is to glorify God and enjoy Him forever." With this agree the four and twenty elders who fall on their faces to worship Him that liveth for ever and ever, saying, "Thou art worthy, O Lord, to receive glory and honour and power: for thou hast created all things, and for thy pleasure they are and were created."

God formed us for His pleasure, and so formed us that we as well as He can in divine communion enjoy the sweet and mysterious mingling of kindred personalities. He meant us to see Him and live with Him and draw our life from His smile. But we have been guilty of that "foul revolt" of which Milton speaks when describing the rebellion of Satan and his hosts. We have broken with God. We have ceased to obey Him or love Him and in guilt and fear have fled as far as possible from His Presence.

Yet who can flee from His Presence when the heaven and the heaven of heavens cannot contain Him? when as the wisdom of Solomon testifies, "the Spirit of the Lord filleth the world?" The omnipresence of the Lord is one thing, and is a solemn fact necessary to His perfection; the *manifest* Presence is another thing altogether, and from that Presence we have fled, like Adam, to hide among the trees of the garden, or like Peter to shrink away crying, "Depart from me, for I am a sinful man, O Lord."

So the life of man upon the earth is a life away from the Presence, wrenched loose from that "blissful center" which is our right and proper dwelling place, our first estate which we kept not, the loss of which is the cause of our unceasing restlessness.

The whole work of God in redemption is to undo the tragic effects of that foul revolt, and to bring us back again into right and eternal relationship with Himself. This required that our sins be disposed of satisfactorily, that a full reconciliation be effected and the way opened for us to return again into conscious communion with God and to live again in the Presence as before. Then by His prevenient working within us He moves us to return. This first comes to our notice when our restless hearts feel a yearning for the Presence of God and we say within ourselves, "I will arise and go to my Father." That is the first step, and as the Chinese sage Lao-tze has said, "The journey of a thousand miles begins with a first step."

The interior journey of the soul from the wilds of sin into the enjoyed Presence of God is beautifully illustrated in the Old Testament tabernacle. The returning sinner first entered the outer court where he offered a blood sacrifice on the brazen altar and washed himself in the laver that stood near it. Then through a veil he passed into the holy place where no natural light could come, but the golden candlestick which spoke of Jesus the Light of the World threw its soft glow over all. There also was the shewbread to tell of Jesus, the Bread of Life, and the altar of incense, a figure of unceasing prayer.

Though the worshipper had enjoyed so much, still he had not yet entered the Presence of God. Another veil separated from the Holy of Holies where above the mercy seat dwelt the very God Himself in awful and glorious manifestation. While the tabernacle stood, only the high priest could enter there, and that but once a year, with blood which he offered for his sins and the sins of the people. It was this last veil which was rent when our Lord gave up the ghost on Calvary, and the sacred writer explains that this rending of the veil opened the way for every worshipper in the world to come by the new and living way straight into the divine Presence.

Everything in the New Testament accords with this Old Testament picture. Ransomed men need no longer pause in fear to enter the Holy of Holies. *God wills that we should push on into His Presence and live our whole life there.* This is to be known to us in conscious experience. It is more than a doctrine to be held, it is a life to be enjoyed every moment of every day.

This Flame of the Presence was the beating heart of the Levitical order. Without it all the appointments of the tabernacle were characters of some unknown language; they had no meaning for Israel or for us. The greatest fact of the tabernacle was that *Jehovah was there*; a Presence was waiting within the veil. Similarly the Presence of God is the central fact of Christianity. At the heart of the Christian message is God Himself waiting for His redeemed children to push in to conscious awareness of His Presence. That type of Christianity which happens now to be the vogue knows this Presence only in theory. It fails to stress the Christian's privilege of present realization. According to its teachings we are in the Presence of God positionally, and nothing is said about the need to experience that Presence actually. The fiery urge that drove men like McCheyne is wholly missing. And the present generation of Christians measures itself by this imperfect rule. Ignoble contentment takes the place of burning zeal. We are satisfied to rest in our *judicial* possessions and for the most part we bother ourselves very little about the absence of personal experience.

Who is this within the veil who dwells in fiery manifestations? It is none other than God Himself, "One God the Father Almighty, Maker of heaven and earth, and of all things visible and invisible," and "One Lord Jesus Christ, the only begotten Son of God; begotten of His Father before all worlds, God of God, Light of Light, Very God of Very God; begotten, not made; being of one substance with the Father," and "the Holy Ghost, the Lord and Giver of life, Who proceedeth from the Father and the Son, Who with the Father and the Son together is worshipped and glorified." Yet this holy Trinity is One God, for "we worship one God in Trinity, and Trinity in Unity; neither confounding the Persons, nor dividing the Substance. For there is one Person of the Father, another of the Son, and another of the Holy Ghost. But the Godhead of the Father, of the Son, and of the Holy Ghost, is all one: the glory equal and the majesty co-eternal." So in part run the ancient creeds, and so the inspired Word declares.

Behind the veil is God, that God after Whom the world, with strange inconsistency, has felt, "if haply they might find Him." He has discovered Himself to some extent in nature, but more perfectly in the Incarnation; now He waits to show Himself in ravishing fulness to the humble of soul and the pure in heart.

The world is perishing for lack of the knowledge of God and the Church is famishing for want of His Presence. The instant cure of most of our religious ills would be to enter the Presence in spiritual experience, to become suddenly aware that we are in God and that God is in us. This would lift us out of our pitiful narrowness and cause our hearts to be enlarged. This would burn away the impurities from our lives as the bugs and fungi were burned away by the fire that dwelt in the bush.

What a broad world to roam in, what a sea to swim in is this God and Father of our Lord Jesus Christ. He is *eternal*, which means that He antedates time and is wholly independent of it. Time began in Him and will end in Him. To it He pays no tribute and from it He suffers no change. He is *immutable*, which means that He has never changed and can never change in any smallest measure. To change He would need to go from better to worse or from worse to better. He cannot do either, for being perfect He cannot become more perfect, and if He were to become less perfect He would be less than God. He is *omniscient*, which means that He knows in one free and effortless act all matter, all spirit, all relationships, all events. He has no past and He has no future. He *is*, and none of the limiting and qualifying terms used of creatures can apply to Him. *Love* and *mercy* and *righteousness* are His, and *holiness* so ineffable that no comparisons or figures will avail to express it. Only fire can give even a remote conception of it. In fire He appeared at the burning bush; in the pillar of fire He dwelt through all the long wilderness journey. The fire that glowed between the wings of the cherubim in the holy place was called the "shekinah," the Presence, through the years of Israel's glory, and when the Old had given place to the New, He came at Pentecost as a fiery flame and rested upon each disciple.

Spinoza wrote of the intellectual love of God, and he had a measure of truth there; but the highest love of God is not intellectual, it is spiritual. God is spirit and only the spirit of man can know Him really. In the deep spirit of a man the fire must glow or his love is not the true love of God. The great of the Kingdom have been those who loved God more than others did. We all know who they have been and gladly pay tribute to the depths and sincerity of their devotion. We have but to pause for a moment and their names come trooping past us smelling of myrrh and aloes and cassia out of the ivory palaces.

Frederick Faber was one whose soul panted after God as the roe pants after the water brook, and the measure in which God revealed Himself to his seeking heart set the good man's whole life afire with a burning adoration rivaling that of the seraphim before the throne. His love for God extended to the three Persons of the Godhead equally, yet he seemed to feel for each One a special kind of love reserved for Him alone. Of God the Father he sings:

Only to sit and think of God, Oh what a joy it is! To think the thought, to breathe the Name; Earth has no higher bliss.

Father of Jesus, love's reward! What rapture will it be, Prostrate before Thy throne to lie, And gaze and gaze on Thee!

His love for the Person of Christ was so intense that it threatened to consume him; it burned within him as a sweet and holy madness and flowed from his lips like molten gold. In one of his sermons he says, "Wherever we turn in the church of God, there is Jesus. He is the beginning, middle and end of everything to us.... There is nothing good, nothing holy, nothing beautiful, nothing joyous which He is not to His servants. No one need be poor, because, if he chooses, he can have Jesus for his own property and possession. No one need be downcast, for Jesus is the joy of heaven, and it is His joy to enter into sorrowful hearts.

We can exaggerate about many things; but we can never exaggerate our obligation to Jesus, or the compassionate abundance of the love of Jesus to us. All our lives long we might talk of Jesus, and yet we should never come to an end of the sweet things that might be said of Him. Eternity will not be long enough to learn all He is, or to praise Him for all He has done, but then, that matters not; for we shall be always with Him, and we desire nothing more." And addressing our Lord directly he says to Him:

I love Thee so, I know not how My transports to control; Thy love is like a burning fire Within my very soul.

Faber's blazing love extended also to the Holy Spirit. Not only in his theology did he acknowledge His deity and full equality with the Father and the Son, but he celebrated it constantly in his songs and in his prayers. He literally pressed his forehead to the ground in his eager fervid worship of the Third Person of the Godhead. In one of his great hymns to the Holy Spirit he sums up his burning devotion thus:

O Spirit, beautiful and dread! My heart is fit to break With love of all Thy tenderness For us poor sinners' sake.

I have risked the tedium of quotation that I might show by pointed example what I have set out to say, viz., that God is so vastly wonderful, so utterly and completely delightful that He can, without anything other than Himself, meet and overflow the deepest demands of our total nature, mysterious and deep as that nature is. Such worship as Faber knew (and he is but one of a great company which no man can number) can never come from a mere doctrinal knowledge of God. Hearts that are "fit to break" with love for the Godhead are those who have been in the Presence and have looked with opened eye upon the majesty of Deity. Men of the breaking hearts had a quality about them not known to or understood by common men. They habitually spoke with spiritual authority. They had been in the Presence of God and they reported what they saw there. They were prophets, not scribes, for the scribe tells us what he has read, and the prophet tells what he has seen.

The distinction is not an imaginary one. Between the scribe who has read and the prophet who has seen there is a difference as wide as the sea. We are today overrun with orthodox scribes, but the prophets, where are they? The hard voice of the scribe sounds over evangelicalism, but the Church waits for the tender voice of the saint who has penetrated the veil and has gazed with inward eye upon the Wonder that is God. And yet, thus to penetrate, to push in sensitive living experience into the holy Presence, is a privilege open to every child of God.

With the veil removed by the rending of Jesus' flesh, with nothing on God's side to prevent us from entering, why do we tarry without? Why do we consent to abide all our days just outside the Holy of Holies and never enter at all to look upon God? We hear the Bridegroom say, "Let me see thy countenance, let me hear thy voice; for sweet is thy voice and thy countenance is comely." We sense that the call is for us, but still we fail to draw near, and the years pass and we grow old and tired in the outer courts of the tabernacle. What doth hinder us?

The answer usually given, simply that we are "cold," will not explain all the facts. There is something more serious than coldness of heart, something that may be back of that coldness and be the cause of its existence. What is it? What but the presence of *a veil in our hearts*? a veil not taken away as the first veil was, but which remains there still shutting out the light and hiding the face of God from us. It is the veil of our fleshly fallen nature living on, unjudged within us, uncrucified and unrepudiated. It is the close-woven veil of the self-life which we have never truly acknowledged, of which we have been secretly ashamed, and which for these reasons we have never brought to the judgment of the cross. It is not too mysterious, this opaque veil, nor is it hard to identify. We have but to look in our own hearts and we shall see it there, sewn and patched and repaired it may be, but there nevertheless, an enemy to our lives and an effective block to our spiritual progress.

This veil is not a beautiful thing and it is not a thing about which we commonly care to talk, but I am addressing the thirsting souls who are determined to follow God, and I know they will not turn back because the way leads temporarily through the blackened hills. The urge of God within them will assure their continuing the pursuit. They will face the facts however unpleasant and endure the cross for the joy set before them. So I am bold to name the threads out of which this inner veil is woven.

It is woven of the fine threads of the self-life, the hyphenated sins of the human spirit. They are not something we do, they are something we *are*, and therein lies both their subtlety and their power.

To be specific, the self-sins are these: self-righteousness, self-pity, self-confidence, self-sufficiency, self-admiration, self-love and a host of others like them. They dwell too deep within us and are too much a part of our natures to come to our attention till the light of God is focused upon them. The grosser manifestations of these sins, egotism, exhibitionism, self-promotion, are strangely tolerated in Christian leaders even in circles of impeccable orthodoxy. They are so much in evidence as actually, for many people, to become identified with the gospel. I trust it is not a cynical observation to say that they appear these days to be a requisite for popularity in some sections of the Church visible. Promoting self under the guise of promoting Christ is currently so common as to excite little notice.

One should suppose that proper instruction in the doctrines of man's depravity and the necessity for justification through the righteousness of Christ alone would deliver us from the power of the self-sins; but it does not work out that way. Self can live unrebuked at the very altar. It can watch the bleeding Victim die and not be in the least affected by what it sees. It can fight for the faith of the Reformers and preach eloquently the creed of salvation by grace, and gain strength by its efforts. To tell all the truth, it seems actually to feed upon orthodoxy and is more at home in a Bible Conference than in a tavern. Our very state of longing after God may afford it an excellent condition under which to thrive and grow.

Self is the opaque veil that hides the Face of God from us. It can be removed only in spiritual experience, never by mere instruction. As well try to instruct leprosy out of our system. There must be a work of God in destruction before we are free. We must invite the cross to do its deadly work within us. We must bring our self-sins to the cross for judgment. We must prepare ourselves for an ordeal of suffering in some measure like that through which our Saviour passed when He suffered under Pontius Pilate.

Let us remember: when we talk of the rending of the veil we are speaking in a figure, and the thought of it is poetical, almost pleasant; but in actuality there is nothing pleasant about it. In human experience that veil is made of living spiritual tissue; it is composed of the sentient, quivering stuff of which our whole beings consist, and to touch it is to touch us where we feel pain. To tear it away is to injure us, to hurt us and make us bleed. To say otherwise is to make the cross no cross and death no death at all. It is never fun to die. To rip through the dear and tender stuff of which life is made can never be anything but deeply painful. Yet that is what the cross did to Jesus and it is what the cross would do to every man to set him free.

Let us beware of tinkering with our inner life in hope ourselves to rend the veil. God must do everything for us. Our part is to yield and trust. We must confess, forsake, repudiate the self-life, and then reckon it crucified. But we must be careful to distinguish lazy "acceptance" from the real work of God. We must insist upon the work being done. We dare not rest content with a neat doctrine of self-crucifixion. That is to imitate Saul and spare the best of the sheep and the oxen.

Insist that the work be done in very truth and it will be done. The cross is rough, and it is deadly, but it is effective. It does not keep its victim hanging there forever. There comes a moment when its work is finished and the suffering victim dies. After that is resurrection glory and power, and the pain is forgotten for joy that the veil is taken away and we have entered in actual spiritual experience the Presence of the living God.

Lord, how excellent are Thy ways, and how devious and dark are the ways of man. Show us how to die, that we may rise again to newness of life. Rend the veil of our self-life from the top down as Thou didst rend the veil of the Temple. We would draw near in full assurance of faith. We would dwell with Thee in daily experience here on this earth so that we may be accustomed to the glory when we enter Thy heaven to dwell with Thee there. In Jesus' name, Amen.

IV *Apprehending God*

O taste and see.—Psa. 34:8

It was Canon Holmes, of India, who more than twenty-five years ago called attention to the inferential character of the average man's faith in God. To most people God is an inference, not a reality. He is a deduction from evidence which they consider adequate; but He remains personally unknown to the individual. "He *must* be," they say, "therefore we believe He is." Others do not go even so far as this; they know of Him only by hearsay. They have never bothered to think the matter out for themselves, but have heard about Him from others, and have put belief in Him into the back of their minds along with the various odds and ends that make up their total creed. To many others God is but an ideal, another name for goodness, or beauty, or truth; or He is law, or life, or the creative impulse back of the phenomena of existence.

These notions about God are many and varied, but they who hold them have one thing in common: they do not know God in personal experience. The possibility of intimate acquaintance with Him has not entered their minds. While admitting His existence they do not think of Him as knowable in the sense that we know things or people.

Christians, to be sure, go further than this, at least in theory. Their creed requires them to believe in the personality of God, and they have been taught to pray, "Our Father, which art in heaven." Now personality and fatherhood carry with them the idea of the possibility of personal acquaintance. This is admitted, I say, in theory, but for millions of Christians, nevertheless, God is no more real than He is to the non-Christian. They go through life trying to love an ideal and be loyal to a mere principle.

Over against all this cloudy vagueness stands the clear scriptural doctrine that God can be known in personal experience. A loving Personality dominates the Bible, walking among the trees of the garden and breathing fragrance over every scene. Always a living Person is present, speaking, pleading, loving, working, and manifesting Himself whenever and wherever His people have the receptivity necessary to receive the manifestation.

The Bible assumes as a self-evident fact that men can know God with at least the same degree of immediacy as they know any other person or thing that comes within the field of their experience. The same terms are used to express the knowledge of God as are used to express knowledge of physical things. "O *taste* and see that the Lord is good." "All thy garments *smell* of myrrh, and aloes, and cassia, out of the ivory palaces." "My sheep *hear* my voice." "Blessed are the pure in heart, for they shall *see* God." These are but four of countless such passages from the Word of God. And more important than any proof text is the fact that the whole import of the Scripture is toward this belief.

What can all this mean except that we have in our hearts organs by means of which we can know God as certainly as we know material things through our familiar five senses? We apprehend the physical world by exercising the faculties given us for the purpose, and we possess spiritual faculties by means of which we can know God and the spiritual world if we will obey the Spirit's urge and begin to use them.

That a saving work must first be done in the heart is taken for granted here. The spiritual faculties of the unregenerate man lie asleep in his nature, unused and for every purpose dead; that is the stroke which has fallen upon us by sin. They may be quickened to active life again by the operation of the Holy Spirit in regeneration; that is one of the immeasurable benefits which come to us through Christ's atoning work on the cross.

But the very ransomed children of God themselves: why do they know so little of that habitual conscious communion with God which the Scriptures seem to offer? The answer is our chronic unbelief. Faith enables our spiritual sense to function. Where faith is defective the result will be inward insensibility and numbness toward spiritual things. This is the condition of vast numbers of Christians today. No proof is necessary to support that statement. We have but to converse with the first Christian we meet or enter the first church we find open to acquire all the proof we need.

A spiritual kingdom lies all about us, enclosing us, embracing us, altogether within reach of our inner selves, waiting for us to recognize it. God Himself is here waiting our response to His Presence. This eternal world will come alive to us the moment we begin to reckon upon its reality.

I have just now used two words which demand definition; or if definition is impossible, I must at least make clear what I mean when I use them. They are "reckon" and "reality."

What do I mean by *reality*? I mean that which has existence apart from any idea any mind may have of it, and which would exist if there were no mind anywhere to entertain a thought of it. That which is real has being in itself. It does not depend upon the observer for its validity.

I am aware that there are those who love to poke fun at the plain man's idea of reality. They are the idealists who spin endless proofs that nothing is real outside of the mind. They are the relativists who like to show that there are no fixed points in the universe from which we can measure anything. They smile down upon us from their lofty intellectual peaks and settle us to their own satisfaction by fastening upon us the reproachful term "absolutist." The Christian is not put out of countenance by this show of contempt. He can smile right back at them, for he knows that there is only One who is Absolute, that is God. But he knows also that the Absolute One has made this world for man's uses, and, while there is nothing fixed or real in the last meaning of the words (the meaning as applied to God) *for every purpose of human life we are permitted to act as if there were*. And every man does act thus except the mentally sick. These unfortunates also have trouble with reality, but they are consistent; they insist upon living in accordance with their ideas of things. They are honest, and it is their very honesty that constitutes them a social problem.

The idealists and relativists are not mentally sick. They prove their soundness by living their lives according to the very notions of reality which they in theory repudiate and by counting upon the very fixed points which they prove are not there. They could earn a lot more respect for their notions if they were willing to live by them; but this they are careful not to do. Their ideas are brain-deep, not life-deep.

Wherever life touches them they repudiate their theories and live like other men.

The Christian is too sincere to play with ideas for their own sake. He takes no pleasure in the mere spinning of gossamer webs for display. All his beliefs are practical. They are geared into his life. By them he lives or dies, stands or falls for this world and for all time to come. From the insincere man he turns away.

The sincere plain man knows that the world is real. He finds it here when he wakes to consciousness, and he knows that he did not think it into being. It was here waiting for him when he came, and he knows that when he prepares to leave this earthly scene it will be here still to bid him good-bye as he departs. By the deep wisdom of life he is wiser than a thousand men who doubt. He stands upon the earth and feels the wind and rain in his face and he knows that they are real. He sees the sun by day and the stars by night. He sees the hot lightning play out of the dark thundercloud. He hears the sounds of nature and the cries of human joy and pain. These he knows are real. He lies down on the cool earth at night and has no fear that it will prove illusory or fail him while he sleeps. In the morning the firm ground will be under him, the blue sky above him and the rocks and trees around him as when he closed his eyes the night before. So he lives and rejoices in a world of reality.

With his five senses he engages this real world. All things necessary to his physical existence he apprehends by the faculties with which he has been equipped by the God who created him and placed him in such a world as this.

Now, by our definition also God is real. He is real in the absolute and final sense that nothing else is. All other reality is contingent upon His. The great Reality is God who is the Author of that lower and dependent reality which makes up the sum of created things, including ourselves. God has objective existence independent of and apart from any notions which we may have concerning Him. The worshipping heart does not create its Object. It finds Him here when it wakes from its moral slumber in the morning of its regeneration.

Another word that must be cleared up is the word *reckon*. This does not mean to visualize or imagine. Imagination is not faith. The two are not only different from, but stand in sharp opposition to, each other. Imagination projects unreal images out of the mind and seeks to attach reality to them. Faith creates nothing; it simply reckons upon that which is already *there*.

God and the spiritual world are real. We can reckon upon them with as much assurance as we reckon upon the familiar world around us. Spiritual things are there (or rather we should say *here*) inviting our attention and challenging our trust.

Our trouble is that we have established bad thought habits. We habitually think of the visible world as real and doubt the reality of any other. We do not deny the existence of the spiritual world but we doubt that it is real in the accepted meaning of the word.

The world of sense intrudes upon our attention day and night for the whole of our lifetime. It is clamorous, insistent and self-demonstrating. It does not appeal to our faith; it is here, assaulting our five senses, demanding to be accepted as real and final. But sin has so clouded the lenses of our hearts that we cannot see that other reality, the City of God, shining around us. The world of sense triumphs. The visible becomes the enemy of the invisible; the temporal, of the eternal. That is the curse inherited by every member of Adam's tragic race.

At the root of the Christian life lies belief in the invisible. The object of the Christian's faith is unseen reality.

Our uncorrected thinking, influenced by the blindness of our natural hearts and the intrusive ubiquity of visible things, tends to draw a contrast between the spiritual and the real; but actually no such contrast exists. The antithesis lies elsewhere: between the real and the imaginary, between the spiritual and the material, between the temporal and the eternal; but between the spiritual and the real, never. The spiritual *is* real.

If we would rise into that region of light and power plainly beckoning us through the Scriptures of truth we must break the evil habit of ignoring the spiritual. We must shift our interest from the seen to the unseen. For the great unseen Reality is God. "He that cometh to God must believe that he is, and that he is a rewarder of them that diligently seek him." This is basic in the life of faith. From there we can rise to unlimited heights. "Ye believe in God," said our Lord Jesus Christ, "believe also in me." Without the first there can be no second.

If we truly want to follow God we must seek to be other-worldly. This I say knowing well that that word has been used with scorn by the sons of this world and applied to the Christian as a badge of reproach. So be it. Every man must choose his world. If we who follow Christ, with all the facts before us and knowing what we are about, deliberately choose the Kingdom of God as our sphere of interest I see no reason why anyone should object. If we lose by it, the loss is our own; if we gain, we rob no one by so doing. The "other world," which is the object of this world's disdain and the subject of the drunkard's mocking song, is our carefully chosen goal and the object of our holiest longing.

But we must avoid the common fault of pushing the "other world" into the future. It is not future, but present. It parallels our familiar physical world, and the doors between the two worlds are open. "Ye are come," says the writer to the Hebrews (and the tense is plainly present), "unto Mount Zion, and unto the city of the living God, the heavenly Jerusalem, and to an innumerable company of angels, to the general assembly and church of the firstborn, which are written in heaven, and to God the Judge of all, and to the spirits of just men made perfect, and to Jesus the mediator of the new covenant, and to the blood of sprinkling, that speaketh better things than that of Abel." All these things are contrasted with "the mount that might be touched" and "the sound of a trumpet and the voice of words" that might be heard. May we not safely conclude that, as the realities of Mount Sinai were apprehended by the senses, so the realities of Mount Zion are to be grasped by the soul? And this not by any trick of the imagination, but in downright actuality. The soul has eyes with which to see and ears with which to hear. Feeble they may be from long disuse, but by the life-giving touch of Christ alive now and capable of sharpest sight and most sensitive hearing.

As we begin to focus upon God the things of the spirit will take shape before our inner eyes. Obedience to the word of Christ will bring an inward revelation of the Godhead (John 14:21-23). It will give acute perception enabling us to see God even as is promised to the pure in heart. A new God consciousness will seize upon us and we shall begin to taste and hear and inwardly feel the God who is our life and our all. There will be seen the constant shining of the light that lighteth every man that cometh into the world. More and more, as our faculties grow sharper and more sure, God will become to us the great All, and His Presence the glory and wonder of our lives.

O God, quicken to life every power within me, that I may lay hold on eternal things. Open my eyes that I may see; give me acute spiritual perception; enable me to taste Thee and know that Thou art good. Make heaven more real to me than any earthly thing has ever been. Amen.

V *The Universal Presence*

> Whither shall I go from thy spirit? or whither shall I flee from thy presence?—*Psa. 139:7*

In all Christian teaching certain basic truths are found, hidden at times, and rather assumed than asserted, but necessary to all truth as the primary colors are found in and necessary to the finished painting. Such a truth is the divine immanence.

God dwells in His creation and is everywhere indivisibly present in all His works. This is boldly taught by prophet and apostle and is accepted by Christian theology generally. That is, it appears in the books, but for some reason it has not sunk into the average Christian's heart so as to become a part of his believing self. Christian teachers shy away from its full implications, and, if they mention it at all, mute it down till it has little meaning. I would guess the reason for this to be the fear of being charged with pantheism; but the doctrine of the divine Presence is definitely not pantheism.

Pantheism's error is too palpable to deceive anyone. It is that God is the sum of all created things. Nature and God are one, so that whoever touches a leaf or a stone touches God. That is of course to degrade the glory of the incorruptible Deity and, in an effort to make all things divine, banish all divinity from the world entirely.

The truth is that while God dwells in His world He is separated from it by a gulf forever impassable. However closely He may be identified with the work of His hands *they* are and must eternally be *other than He*, and He is and must be antecedent to and independent of them. He is transcendent above all His works even while He is immanent within them.

What now does the divine immanence mean in direct Christian experience? It means simply that *God is here*. Wherever we are, God is here. There is no place, there can be no place, where He is not. Ten million intelligences standing at as many points in space and separated by incomprehensible distances can each one say with equal truth, God is here. No point is nearer to God than any other point. It is exactly as near to God from any place as it is from any other place. No one is in mere distance any further from or any nearer to God than any other person is.

These are truths believed by every instructed Christian. It remains for us to think on them and pray over them until they begin to glow within us.

"In the beginning God." Not *matter*, for matter is not self-causing. It requires an antecedent cause, and God is that Cause. Not *law*, for law is but a name for the course which all creation follows. That course had to be planned, and the Planner is God. Not *mind*, for mind also is a created thing and must have a Creator back of it. In the beginning God, the uncaused Cause of matter, mind and law. There we must begin.

Adam sinned and, in his panic, frantically tried to do the impossible: he tried to hide from the Presence of God. David also must have had wild thoughts of trying to escape from the Presence, for he wrote, "Whither shall I go from thy spirit? or whither shall I flee from thy presence?" Then he proceeded through one of his most beautiful psalms to celebrate the glory of the divine immanence. "If I ascend up into heaven, thou art there: if I make my bed in hell, behold, thou art there. If I take the wings of the morning, and dwell in the uttermost parts of the sea; even there shall thy hand lead me, and thy right hand shall hold me." And he knew that God's *being* and God's *seeing* are the same, that the seeing Presence had been with him even before he was born, watching the mystery of unfolding life. Solomon exclaimed, "But will God indeed dwell on the earth? behold the heaven and the heaven of heavens cannot contain thee: how much less this house which I have builded." Paul assured the Athenians that "God is not far from any one of us: for in him we live, and move, and have our being."

If God is present at every point in space, if we cannot go where He is not, cannot even conceive of a place where He is not, why then has not that Presence become the one universally celebrated fact of the world? The patriarch Jacob, "in the waste howling wilderness," gave the answer to that question. He saw a vision of God and cried out in wonder, "Surely the Lord is in this place; and I knew it not." Jacob had never been for one small division of a moment outside the circle of that all-pervading Presence. But he knew it not. That was his trouble, and it is ours. Men do not know that God is here. What a difference it would make if they knew.

The Presence and the manifestation of the Presence are not the same. There can be the one without the other. God is here when we are wholly unaware of it. He is *manifest* only when and as we are aware of His Presence. On our part there must be surrender to the Spirit of God, for His work it is to show us the Father and the Son. If we co-operate with Him in loving obedience God will manifest Himself to us, and that manifestation will be the difference between a nominal Christian life and a life radiant with the light of His face.

Always, everywhere God is present, and always He seeks to discover Himself. To each one he would reveal not only that He is, but *what* He is as well. He did not have to be persuaded to discover Himself to Moses. "And the Lord descended in the cloud, and stood with him there, and proclaimed the name of the Lord." He not only made a verbal proclamation of His nature but He revealed His very Self to Moses so that the skin of Moses' face shone with the supernatural light. It will be a great moment for some of us when we begin to believe that God's promise of self-revelation is literally true: that He promised much, but promised no more than He intends to fulfill.

Our pursuit of God is successful just because He is forever seeking to manifest Himself to us. The revelation of God to any man is not God coming from a distance upon a time to pay a brief and momentous visit to the man's soul. Thus to think of it is to misunderstand it all. The approach of God to the soul or of the soul to God is not to be thought of in spatial terms at all. There is no idea of physical distance involved in the concept. It is not a matter of miles but of experience.

To speak of being near to or far from God is to use language in a sense always understood when applied to our ordinary human relationships. A man may say, "I feel that my son is coming nearer to me as he gets older," and yet that son has lived by his father's side since he was born and has never been away from home more than a day or so in his entire life. What then can the father mean? Obviously he is speaking of *experience*. He means that the boy is coming to know him more intimately and with deeper understanding, that the barriers of thought and feeling between the two are disappearing, that father and son are becoming more closely united in mind and heart.

So when we sing, "Draw me nearer, nearer, blessed Lord," we are not thinking of the nearness of place, but of the nearness of relationship. It is for increasing degrees of awareness that we pray, for a more perfect consciousness of the divine Presence. We need never shout across the spaces to an absent God. He is nearer than our own soul, closer than our most secret thoughts.

Why do some persons "find" God in a way that others do not? Why does God manifest His Presence to some and let multitudes of others struggle along in the half-light of imperfect Christian experience? Of course the will of God is the same for all. He has no favorites within His household. All He has ever done for any of His children He will do for all of His children. The difference lies not with God but with us.

Pick at random a score of great saints whose lives and testimonies are widely known. Let them be Bible characters or well known Christians of post-Biblical times. You will be struck instantly with the fact that the saints were not alike. Sometimes the unlikenesses were so great as to be positively glaring. How different for example was Moses from Isaiah; how different was Elijah from David; how unlike each other were John and Paul, St. Francis and Luther, Finney and Thomas à Kempis. The differences are as wide as human life itself: differences of race, nationality, education, temperament, habit and personal qualities. Yet they all walked, each in his day, upon a high road of spiritual living far above the common way.

Their differences must have been incidental and in the eyes of God of no significance. In some vital quality they must have been alike. What was it?

I venture to suggest that the one vital quality which they had in common was *spiritual receptivity*. Something in them was open to heaven, something which urged them Godward. Without attempting anything like a profound analysis I shall say simply that they had spiritual awareness and that they went on to cultivate it until it became the biggest thing in their lives. They differed from the average person in that when they felt the inward longing they *did something about it*. They acquired the lifelong habit of spiritual response. They were not disobedient to the heavenly vision. As David put it neatly, "When thou saidst, Seek ye my face; my heart said unto thee, Thy face, Lord, will I seek."

As with everything good in human life, back of this receptivity is God. The sovereignty of God is here, and is felt even by those who have not placed particular stress upon it theologically. The pious Michael Angelo confessed this in a sonnet:

My unassisted heart is barren clay, That of its native self can nothing feed: Of good and pious works Thou art the seed, That quickens only where Thou sayest it may: Unless Thou show to us Thine own true way No man can find it: Father! Thou must lead.

These words will repay study as the deep and serious testimony of a great Christian.

Important as it is that we recognize God working in us, I would yet warn against a too-great preoccupation with the thought. It is a sure road to sterile passivity. God will not hold us responsible to understand the mysteries of election, predestination and the divine sovereignty. The best and safest way to deal with these truths is to raise our eyes to God and in deepest reverence say, "O Lord, Thou knowest." Those things belong to the deep and mysterious Profound of God's omniscience. Prying into them may make theologians, but it will never make saints.

Receptivity is not a single thing; it is a compound rather, a blending of several elements within the soul. It is an affinity for, a bent toward, a sympathetic response to, a desire to have. From this it may be gathered that it can be present in degrees, that we may have little or more or less, depending upon the individual. It may be increased by exercise or destroyed by neglect. It is not a sovereign and irresistible force which comes upon us as a seizure from above. It is a gift of God, indeed, but one which must be recognized and cultivated as any other gift if it is to realize the purpose for which it was given.

Failure to see this is the cause of a very serious breakdown in modern evangelicalism. The idea of cultivation and exercise, so dear to the saints of old, has now no place in our total religious picture. It is too slow, too common. We now demand glamour and fast flowing dramatic action. A generation of Christians reared among push buttons and automatic machines is impatient of slower and less direct methods of reaching their goals. We have been trying to apply machine-age methods to our relations with God. We read our chapter, have our short devotions and rush away, hoping to make up for our deep inward bankruptcy by attending another gospel meeting or listening to another thrilling story told by a religious adventurer lately returned from afar.

The tragic results of this spirit are all about us. Shallow lives, hollow religious philosophies, the preponderance of the element of fun in gospel meetings, the glorification of men, trust in religious externalities, quasi-religious fellowships, salesmanship methods, the mistaking of dynamic personality for the power of the Spirit: these and such as these are the symptoms of an evil disease, a deep and serious malady of the soul.

For this great sickness that is upon us no one person is responsible, and no Christian is wholly free from blame. We have all contributed, directly or indirectly, to this sad state of affairs. We have been too blind to see, or too timid to speak out, or too self-satisfied to desire anything better than the poor average diet with which others appear satisfied. To put it differently, we have accepted one another's notions, copied one another's lives and made one another's experiences the model for our own. And for a generation the trend has been downward. Now we have reached a low place of sand and burnt wire grass and, worst of all, we have made the Word of Truth conform to our experience and accepted this low plane as the very pasture of the blessed.

It will require a determined heart and more than a little courage to wrench ourselves loose from the grip of our times and return to Biblical ways. But it can be done. Every now and then in the past Christians have had to do it. History has recorded several large-scale returns led by such men as St. Francis, Martin Luther and George Fox. Unfortunately there seems to be no Luther or Fox on the horizon at present. Whether or not another such return may be expected before the coming of Christ is a question upon which Christians are not fully agreed, but that is not of too great importance to us now.

What God in His sovereignty may yet do on a world-scale I do not claim to know: but what He will do for the plain man or woman who seeks His face I believe I do know and can tell others. Let any man turn to God in earnest, let him begin to exercise himself unto godliness, let him seek to develop his powers of spiritual receptivity by trust and obedience and humility, and the results will exceed anything he may have hoped in his leaner and weaker days.

Any man who by repentance and a sincere return to God will break himself out of the mold in which he has been held, and will go to the Bible itself for his spiritual standards, will be delighted with what he finds there.

Let us say it again: The Universal Presence is a fact. God is here. The whole universe is alive with His life. And He is no strange or foreign God, but the familiar Father of our Lord Jesus Christ whose love has for these thousands of years enfolded the sinful race of men. And always He is trying to get our attention, to reveal Himself to us, to communicate with us. We have within us the ability to know Him if we will but respond to His overtures. (And this we call pursuing God!) We will know Him in increasing degree as our receptivity becomes more perfect by faith and love and practice.

O God and Father, I repent of my sinful preoccupation with visible things. The world has been too much with me. Thou hast been here and I knew it not. I have been blind to Thy Presence. Open my eyes that I may behold Thee in and around me. For Christ's sake, Amen.

VI *The Speaking Voice*

> In the beginning was the Word, and the Word was with God,
> and the Word was God.—*John 1:1*

An intelligent plain man, untaught in the truths of Christianity, coming upon this text, would likely conclude that John meant to teach that it is the nature of God to speak, to communicate His thoughts to others. And he would be right. A word is a medium by which thoughts are expressed, and the application of term to the Eternal Son leads us to believe that self-expression is inherent in the Godhead, that God is forever seeking to speak Himself out to His creation. The whole Bible supports the idea. God is speaking. Not God spoke, but *God is speaking*. He is by His nature continuously articulate. He fills the world with His speaking Voice.

One of the great realities with which we have to deal is the Voice of God in His world. The briefest and only satisfying cosmogony is this: "He spake and it was done." The *why* of natural law is the living Voice of God immanent in His creation. And this word of God which brought all worlds into being cannot be understood to mean the Bible, for it is not a written or printed word at all, but the expression of the will of God spoken into the structure of all things. This word of God is the breath of God filling the world with living potentiality. The Voice of God is the most powerful force in nature, indeed the only force in nature, for all energy is here only because the power-filled Word is being spoken.

The Bible is the written word of God, and because it is written it is confined and limited by the necessities of ink and paper and leather. The Voice of God, however, is alive and free as the sovereign God is free. "The words that I speak unto you, they are spirit, and they are life." The life is in the speaking words. God's word in the Bible can have power only because it corresponds to God's word in the universe. It is the present Voice which makes the written Word all-powerful. Otherwise it would lie locked in slumber within the covers of a book.

We take a low and primitive view of things when we conceive of God at the creation coming into physical contact with things, shaping and fitting and building like a carpenter. The Bible teaches otherwise: "By the word of the Lord were the heavens made; and all the host of them by the breath of his mouth.... For he spake, and it was done; he commanded, and it stood fast." "Through faith we understand that the worlds were framed by the word of God." Again we must remember that God is referring here not to His written Word, but to His speaking Voice. His world-filling Voice is meant, that Voice which antedates the Bible by uncounted centuries, that Voice which has not been silent since the dawn of creation, but is sounding still throughout the full far reaches of the universe.

The Word of God is quick and powerful. In the beginning He spoke to nothing, and it became *something*. Chaos heard it and became order, darkness heard it and became light. "And God said—and it was so." These twin phrases, as cause and effect, occur throughout the Genesis story of the creation. The *said* accounts for the *so*. The *so* is the *said* put into the continuous present.

That God is here and that He is speaking—these truths are back of all other Bible truths; without them there could be no revelation at all. God did not write a book and send it by messenger to be read at a distance by unaided minds. He spoke a Book and lives in His spoken words, constantly speaking His words and causing the power of them to persist across the years. God breathed on clay and it became a man; He breathes on men and they become clay. "Return ye children of men" was the word spoken at the Fall by which God decreed the death of every man, and no added word has He needed to speak. The sad procession of mankind across the face of the earth from birth to the grave is proof that His original Word was enough.

We have not given sufficient attention to that deep utterance in the Book of John, "That was the true Light, which lighteth every man that cometh into the world." Shift the punctuation around as we will and the truth is still there: the Word of God affects the hearts of all men as light in the soul. In the hearts of all men the light shines, the Word sounds, and there is no escaping them. Something like this would of necessity be so if God is alive and in His world. And John says that it is so. Even those persons who have never heard of the Bible have still been preached to with sufficient clarity to remove every excuse from their hearts forever. "Which show the work of the law written in their hearts, their conscience also bearing witness, and their thoughts the mean while either accusing or else excusing one another." "For the invisible things of him from the creation of the world are clearly seen, being understood by the things that are made, even his eternal power and Godhead; so that they are without excuse."

This universal Voice of God was by the ancient Hebrews often called Wisdom, and was said to be everywhere sounding and searching throughout the earth, seeking some response from the sons of men. The eighth chapter of the Book of Proverbs begins, "Doth not wisdom cry? and understanding put forth her voice?" The writer then pictures wisdom as a beautiful woman standing "in the top of the high places, by the way in the places of the paths." She sounds her voice from every quarter so that no one may miss hearing it. "Unto you, O men, I call; and my voice is to the sons of men." Then she pleads for the simple and the foolish to give ear to her words. It is spiritual response for which this Wisdom of God is pleading, a response which she has always sought and is but rarely able to secure. The tragedy is that our eternal welfare depends upon our hearing, and we have trained our ears not to hear.

This universal Voice has ever sounded, and it has often troubled men even when they did not understand the source of their fears. Could it be that this Voice distilling like a living mist upon the hearts of men has been the undiscovered cause of the troubled conscience and the longing for immortality confessed by millions since the dawn of recorded history? We need not fear to face up to this. The speaking Voice is a fact. How men have reacted to it is for any observer to note.

When God spoke out of heaven to our Lord, self-centered men who heard it explained it by natural causes: they said, "It thundered." This habit of explaining the Voice by appeals to natural law is at the very root of modern science. In the living breathing cosmos there is a mysterious Something, too wonderful, too awful for any mind to understand. The believing man does not claim to understand. He falls to his knees and whispers, "God." The man of earth kneels also, but not to worship. He kneels to examine, to search, to find the cause and the how of things. Just now we happen to be living in a secular age. Our thought habits are those of the scientist, not those of the worshipper. We are more likely to explain than to adore. "It thundered," we exclaim, and go our earthly way. But still the Voice sounds and searches. The order and life of the world depend upon that Voice, but men are mostly too busy or too stubborn to give attention.

Everyone of us has had experiences which we have not been able to explain: a sudden sense of loneliness, or a feeling of wonder or awe in the face of the universal vastness. Or we have had a fleeting visitation of light like an illumination from some other sun, giving us in a quick flash an assurance that we are from another world, that our origins are divine. What we saw there, or felt, or heard, may have been contrary to all that we had been taught in the schools and at wide variance with all our former beliefs and opinions. We were forced to suspend our acquired doubts while, for a moment, the clouds were rolled back and we saw and heard for ourselves. Explain such things as we will, I think we have not been fair to the facts until we allow at least the possibility that such experiences may arise from the Presence of God in the world and His persistent effort to communicate with mankind. Let us not dismiss such an hypothesis too flippantly.

It is my own belief (and here I shall not feel bad if no one follows me) that every good and beautiful thing which man has produced in the world has been the result of his faulty and sin-blocked response to the creative Voice sounding over the earth. The moral philosophers who dreamed their high dreams of virtue, the religious thinkers who speculated about God and immortality, the poets and artists who created out of common stuff pure and lasting beauty: how can we explain them? It is not enough to say simply, "It was genius." What then is genius? Could it be that a genius is a man haunted by the speaking Voice, laboring and striving like one possessed to achieve ends which he only vaguely understands? That the great man may have missed God in his labors, that he may even have spoken or written against God does not destroy the idea I am advancing. God's redemptive revelation in the Holy Scriptures is necessary to saving faith and peace with God. Faith in a risen Saviour is necessary if the vague stirrings toward immortality are to bring us to restful and satisfying communion with God. To me this is a plausible explanation of all that is best out of Christ. But you can be a good Christian and not accept my thesis.

The Voice of God is a friendly Voice. No one need fear to listen to it unless he has already made up his mind to resist it. The blood of Jesus has covered not only the human race but all creation as well. "And having made peace through the blood of his cross, by him to reconcile all things unto himself; by him, I say, whether they be things in earth, or things in heaven." We may safely preach a friendly Heaven. The heavens as well as the earth are filled with the good will of Him that dwelt in the bush. The perfect blood of atonement secures this forever.

Whoever will listen will hear the speaking Heaven. This is definitely not the hour when men take kindly to an exhortation to *listen*, for listening is not today a part of popular religion. We are at the opposite end of the pole from there. Religion has accepted the monstrous heresy that noise, size, activity and bluster make a man dear to God. But we may take heart. To a people caught in the tempest of the last great conflict God says, "Be still, and know that I am God," and still He says it, as if He means to tell us that our strength and safety lie not in noise but in silence.

It is important that we get still to wait on God. And it is best that we get alone, preferably with our Bible outspread before us. Then if we will we may draw near to God and begin to hear Him speak to us in our hearts. I think for the average person the progression will be something like this: First a sound as of a Presence walking in the garden. Then a voice, more intelligible, but still far from clear. Then the happy moment when the Spirit begins to illuminate the Scriptures, and that which had been only a sound, or at best a voice, now becomes an intelligible word, warm and intimate and clear as the word of a dear friend. Then will come life and light, and best of all, ability to see and rest in and embrace Jesus Christ as Saviour and Lord and All.

The Bible will never be a living Book to us until we are convinced that God is articulate in His universe. To jump from a dead, impersonal world to a dogmatic Bible is too much for most people. They may admit that they *should* accept the Bible as the Word of God, and they may try to think of it as such, but they find it impossible to believe that the words there on the page are actually for them. A man may *say*, "These words are addressed to me," and yet in his heart not feel and know that they are. He is the victim of a divided psychology. He tries to think of God as mute everywhere else and vocal only in a book.

I believe that much of our religious unbelief is due to a wrong conception of and a wrong feeling for the Scriptures of Truth. A silent God suddenly began to speak in a book and when the book was finished lapsed back into silence again forever. Now we read the book as the record of what God said when He was for a brief time in a speaking mood. With notions like that in our heads how can we believe? The facts are that God is not silent, has never been silent. It is the nature of God to speak. The second Person of the Holy Trinity is called the *Word*. The Bible is the inevitable outcome of God's continuous speech. It is the infallible declaration of His mind for us put into our familiar human words.

I think a new world will arise out of the religious mists when we approach our Bible with the idea that it is not only a book which was once spoken, but a book which is *now speaking*. The prophets habitually said, "Thus *saith* the Lord." They meant their hearers to understand that God's speaking is in the continuous present. We may use the past tense properly to indicate that at a certain time a certain word of God was spoken, but a word of God once spoken continues to be spoken, as a child once born continues to be alive, or a world once created continues to exist. And those are but imperfect illustrations, for children die and worlds burn out, but the Word of our God endureth forever.

If you would follow on to know the Lord, come at once to the open Bible expecting it to speak to you. Do not come with the notion that it is a *thing* which you may push around at your convenience. It is more than a thing, it is a voice, a word, the very Word of the living God.

Lord, teach me to listen. The times are noisy and my ears are weary with the thousand raucous sounds which continuously assault them. Give me the spirit of the boy Samuel when he said to Thee, "Speak, for thy servant heareth." Let me hear Thee speaking in my heart. Let me get used to the sound of Thy Voice, that its tones may be familiar when the sounds of earth die away and the only sound will be the music of Thy speaking Voice. Amen.

VII *The Gaze of the Soul*

> Looking unto Jesus the author and finisher of our faith.—*Heb. 12:2*

Let us think of our intelligent plain man mentioned in chapter six coming for the first time to the reading of the Scriptures. He approaches the Bible without any previous knowledge of what it contains. He is wholly without prejudice; he has nothing to prove and nothing to defend.

Such a man will not have read long until his mind begins to observe certain truths standing out from the page. They are the spiritual principles behind the record of God's dealings with men, and woven into the writings of holy men as they "were moved by the Holy Ghost." As he reads on he might want to number these truths as they become clear to him and make a brief summary under each number. These summaries will be the tenets of his Biblical creed. Further reading will not affect these points except to enlarge and strengthen them. Our man is finding out what the Bible actually teaches.

High up on the list of things which the Bible teaches will be the doctrine of *faith*. The place of weighty importance which the Bible gives to faith will be too plain for him to miss. He will very likely conclude: Faith is all-important in the life of the soul. Without faith it is impossible to please God. Faith will get me anything, take me anywhere in the Kingdom of God, but without faith there can be no approach to God, no forgiveness, no deliverance, no salvation, no communion, no spiritual life at all.

By the time our friend has reached the eleventh chapter of Hebrews the eloquent encomium which is there pronounced upon faith will not seem strange to him. He will have read Paul's powerful defense of faith in his Roman and Galatian epistles. Later if he goes on to study church history he will understand the amazing power in the teachings of the Reformers as they showed the central place of faith in the Christian religion.

Now if faith is so vitally important, if it is an indispensable *must* in our pursuit of God, it is perfectly natural that we should be deeply concerned over whether or not we possess this most precious gift. And our minds being what they are, it is inevitable that sooner or later we should get around to inquiring after the nature of faith. What *is* faith? would lie close to the question, Do I *have* faith? and would demand an answer if it were anywhere to be found.

Almost all who preach or write on the subject of faith have much the same things to say concerning it. They tell us that it is believing a promise, that it is taking God at His word, that it is reckoning the Bible to be true and stepping out upon it. The rest of the book or sermon is usually taken up with stories of persons who have had their prayers answered as a result of their faith. These answers are mostly direct gifts of a practical and temporal nature such as health, money, physical protection or success in business. Or if the teacher is of a philosophic turn of mind he may take another course and lose us in a welter of metaphysics or snow us under with psychological jargon as he defines and re-defines, paring the slender hair of faith thinner and thinner till it disappears in gossamer shavings at last. When he is finished we get up disappointed and go out "by that same door where in we went." Surely there must be something better than this.

In the Scriptures there is practically no effort made to define faith. Outside of a brief fourteen-word definition in Hebrews 11:1, I know of no Biblical definition, and even there faith is defined functionally, not philosophically; that is, it is a statement of what faith is *in operation*, *not* what it is *in essence*. It assumes the presence of faith and shows what it results in, rather than what it is. We will be wise to go just that far and attempt to go no further. We are told from whence it comes and by what means: "Faith is a gift of God," and "Faith cometh by hearing, and hearing by the word of God." This much is clear, and, to paraphrase Thomas à Kempis, "I had rather exercise faith than know the definition thereof."

From here on, when the words "faith is" or their equivalent occur in this chapter I ask that they be understood to refer to what faith is in operation as exercised by a believing man. Right here we drop the notion of definition and think about faith as it may be experienced in action. The complexion of our thoughts will be practical, not theoretical.

In a dramatic story in the Book of Numbers faith is seen in action. Israel became discouraged and spoke against God, and the Lord sent fiery serpents among them. "And they bit the people; and much people of Israel died." Then Moses sought the Lord for them and He heard and gave them a remedy against the bite of the serpents. He commanded Moses to make a serpent of brass and put it upon a pole in sight of all the people, "and it shall come to pass, that everyone that is bitten, when he looketh upon it, shall live." Moses obeyed, "and it came to pass, that if a serpent had bitten any man, when he beheld the serpent of brass, he lived" (Num. 21:4-9).

In the New Testament this important bit of history is interpreted for us by no less an authority than our Lord Jesus Christ Himself. He is explaining to His hearers how they may be saved. He tells them that it is by believing. Then to make it clear He refers to this incident in the Book of Numbers. "As Moses lifted up the serpent in the wilderness, even so must the Son of man be lifted up: that whosoever believeth in him should not perish, but have eternal life" (John 3:14-15).

Our plain man in reading this would make an important discovery. He would notice that "look" and "believe" were synonymous terms. "Looking" on the Old Testament serpent is identical with "believing" on the New Testament Christ. That is, the *looking* and the *believing* are the same thing. And he would understand that while Israel looked with their external eyes, believing is done with the heart. I think he would conclude that *faith is the gaze of a soul upon a saving God.*

When he had seen this he would remember passages he had read before, and their meaning would come flooding over him. "They looked unto him, and were lightened: and their faces were not ashamed" (Psa. 34:5). "Unto thee lift I up mine eyes, O thou that dwellest in the heavens. Behold, as the eyes of servants look unto the hand of their masters, and as the eyes of a maiden unto the hand of her mistress; so our eyes wait upon the Lord our God, until that he have mercy upon us" (Psa. 123:1-2). Here the man seeking mercy looks straight at the God of mercy and never takes his eyes away from Him till mercy is granted. And our Lord Himself looked always at God. "Looking up to heaven, he blessed, and brake, and gave the bread to his disciples" (Matt. 14:19).

Indeed Jesus taught that He wrought His works by always keeping His inward eyes upon His Father. His power lay in His continuous look at God (John 5:19-21).

In full accord with the few texts we have quoted is the whole tenor of the inspired Word. It is summed up for us in the Hebrew epistle when we are instructed to run life's race "looking unto Jesus the author and finisher of our faith." From all this we learn that faith is not a once-done act, but a continuous gaze of the heart at the Triune God.

Believing, then, is directing the heart's attention to Jesus. It is lifting the mind to "behold the Lamb of God," and never ceasing that beholding for the rest of our lives. At first this may be difficult, but it becomes easier as we look steadily at His wondrous Person, quietly and without strain. Distractions may hinder, but once the heart is committed to Him, after each brief excursion away from Him the attention will return again and rest upon Him like a wandering bird coming back to its window.

I would emphasize this one committal, this one great volitional act which establishes the heart's intention to gaze forever upon Jesus. God takes this intention for our choice and makes what allowances He must for the thousand distractions which beset us in this evil world. He knows that we have set the direction of our hearts toward Jesus, and we can know it too, and comfort ourselves with the knowledge that a habit of soul is forming which will become after a while a sort of spiritual reflex requiring no more conscious effort on our part.

Faith is the least self-regarding of the virtues. It is by its very nature scarcely conscious of its own existence. Like the eye which sees everything in front of it and never sees itself, faith is occupied with the Object upon which it rests and pays no attention to itself at all. While we are looking at God we do not see ourselves—blessed riddance. The man who has struggled to purify himself and has had nothing but repeated failures will experience real relief when he stops tinkering with his soul and looks away to the perfect One. While he looks at Christ the very things he has so long been trying to do will be getting done within him. It will be God working in him to will and to do.

Faith is not in itself a meritorious act; the merit is in the One toward Whom it is directed. Faith is a redirecting of our sight, a getting out of the focus of our own vision and getting God into focus. Sin has twisted our vision inward and made it self-regarding. Unbelief has put self where God should be, and is perilously close to the sin of Lucifer who said, "I will set my throne above the throne of God." Faith looks *out* instead of *in* and the whole life falls into line.

All this may seem too simple. But we have no apology to make. To those who would seek to climb into heaven after help or descend into hell God says, "The word is nigh thee, even the word of faith." The word induces us to lift up our eyes unto the Lord and the blessed work of faith begins.

When we lift our inward eyes to gaze upon God we are sure to meet friendly eyes gazing back at us, for it is written that the eyes of the Lord run to and fro throughout all the earth. The sweet language of experience is "Thou God seest me." When the eyes of the soul looking out meet the eyes of God looking in, heaven has begun right here on this earth.

"When all my endeavour is turned toward Thee because all Thy endeavour is turned toward me; when I look unto Thee alone with all my attention, nor ever turn aside the eyes of my mind, because Thou dost enfold me with Thy constant regard; when I direct my love toward Thee alone because Thou, who art Love's self hast turned Thee toward me alone. And what, Lord, is my life, save that embrace wherein Thy delightsome sweetness doth so lovingly enfold me?"[1] So wrote Nicholas of Cusa four hundred years ago.

I should like to say more about this old man of God. He is not much known today anywhere among Christian believers, and among current Fundamentalists he is known not at all. I feel that we could gain much from a little acquaintance with men of his spiritual flavor and the school of Christian thought which they represent. Christian literature, to be accepted and approved by the evangelical leaders of our times, must follow very closely the same train of thought, a kind of "party line" from which it is scarcely safe to depart. A half-century of this in America has made us smug and content. We imitate each other with

---

1   Nicholas of Cusa, *The Vision of God*, E. P. Dutton & Co., Inc., New York, 1928. This and the following quotations used by kind permission of the publishers.

slavish devotion and our most strenuous efforts are put forth to try to say the same thing that everyone around us is saying—and yet to find an excuse for saying it, some little safe variation on the approved theme or, if no more, at least a new illustration.

Nicholas was a true follower of Christ, a lover of the Lord, radiant and shining in his devotion to the Person of Jesus. His theology was orthodox, but fragrant and sweet as everything about Jesus might properly be expected to be. His conception of eternal life, for instance, is beautiful in itself and, if I mistake not, is nearer in spirit to John 17:3 than that which is current among us today. Life eternal, says Nicholas, is "nought other than that blessed regard wherewith Thou never ceasest to behold me, yea, even the secret places of my soul. With Thee, to behold is to give life; 'tis unceasingly to impart sweetest love of Thee; 'tis to inflame me to love of Thee by love's imparting, and to feed me by inflaming, and by feeding to kindle my yearning, and by kindling to make me drink of the dew of gladness, and by drinking to infuse in me a fountain of life, and by infusing to make it increase and endure."[2]

Now, if faith is the gaze of the heart at God, and if this gaze is but the raising of the inward eyes to meet the all-seeing eyes of God, then it follows that it is one of the easiest things possible to do. It would be like God to make the most vital thing easy and place it within the range of possibility for the weakest and poorest of us.

Several conclusions may fairly be drawn from all this. The simplicity of it, for instance. Since believing is looking, it can be done without special equipment or religious paraphernalia. God has seen to it that the one life-and-death essential can never be subject to the caprice of accident. Equipment can break down or get lost, water can leak away, records can be destroyed by fire, the minister can be delayed or the church burn down. All these are external to the soul and are subject to accident or mechanical failure: but *looking* is of the heart and can be done successfully by any man standing up or kneeling down or lying in his last agony a thousand miles from any church.

Since believing is looking it can be done *any time*. No season is superior to another season for this sweetest of all acts. God never made salvation depend upon new moons nor holy days or sabbaths. A man is not nearer to Christ on Easter Sunday than he is, say, on Saturday, August 3, or Monday, October 4. As long as Christ sits on the mediatorial throne every day is a good day and all days are days of salvation.

Neither does *place* matter in this blessed work of believing God. Lift your heart and let it rest upon Jesus and you are instantly in a sanctuary though it be a Pullman berth or a factory or a kitchen. You can see God from anywhere if your mind is set to love and obey Him.

Now, someone may ask, "Is not this of which you speak for special persons such as monks or ministers who have by the nature of their calling more time to devote to quiet meditation? I am a busy worker and have little time to spend alone." I am happy to say that the life I describe is for everyone of God's children regardless of calling. It is, in fact, happily practiced every day by many hard working persons and is beyond the reach of none.

Many have found the secret of which I speak and, without giving much thought to what is going on within them, constantly practice this habit of inwardly gazing upon God. They know that something inside their hearts sees God. Even when they are compelled to withdraw their conscious attention in order to engage in earthly affairs there is within them a secret communion always going on. Let their attention but be released for a moment from necessary business and it flies at once to God again. This has been the testimony of many Christians, so many that even as I state it thus I have a feeling that I am quoting, though from whom or from how many I cannot possibly know.

I do not want to leave the impression that the ordinary means of grace have no value. They most assuredly have. Private prayer should be practiced by every Christian. Long periods of Bible meditation will purify our gaze and direct it; church attendance will enlarge our outlook and increase our love for others. Service and work and activity; all are good and should be engaged in by every Christian. But at the bottom of all these things, giving meaning to them, will be the inward habit of beholding God. A new set of eyes (so to speak) will develop within us enabling us to be looking at God while our outward eyes are seeing the scenes of this passing world.

Someone may fear that we are magnifying private religion out of all proportion, that the "us" of the New Testament is being displaced by a selfish "I." Has it ever occurred to you that one hundred pianos all tuned to the same fork are automatically tuned to each other? They are of one accord by being tuned, not to each other, but to another standard to which each one must individually bow. So one hundred worshippers met together, each one looking away to Christ, are in heart nearer to each other than they could possibly be were they to become "unity" conscious and turn their eyes away from God to strive for closer fellowship. Social religion is perfected when private religion is purified. The body becomes stronger as its members become healthier. The whole Church of God gains when the members that compose it begin to seek a better and a higher life.

All the foregoing presupposes true repentance and a full committal of the life to God. It is hardly necessary to mention this, for only persons who have made such a committal will have read this far.

When the habit of inwardly gazing Godward becomes fixed within us we shall be ushered onto a new level of spiritual life more in keeping with the promises of God and the mood of the New Testament. The Triune God will be our dwelling place even while our feet walk the low road of simple duty here among men. We will have found life's *summum bonum* indeed. "There is the source of all delights that can be desired; not only can nought better be thought out by men and angels, but nought better can exist in mode of being! For it is the absolute maximum of every rational desire, than which a greater cannot be."[3]

O Lord, I have heard a good word inviting me to look away to Thee and be satisfied. My heart longs to respond, but sin has clouded my vision till I see Thee but dimly. Be pleased to cleanse me in Thine own precious blood, and make me inwardly pure, so that I may with unveiled eyes gaze upon Thee all the days of my earthly pilgrimage. Then shall I be prepared to behold Thee in full splendor in the day when Thou shalt appear to be glorified in Thy saints and admired in all them that believe. Amen.

3 *The Vision of God*

VIII *Restoring the Creator-creature Relation*

> Be thou exalted, O God, above the heavens; let thy glory be above all the earth.—*Psa. 57:5*

It is a truism to say that order in nature depends upon right relationships; to achieve harmony each thing must be in its proper position relative to each other thing. In human life it is not otherwise.

I have hinted before in these chapters that the cause of all our human miseries is a radical moral dislocation, an upset in our relation to God and to each other. For whatever else the Fall may have been, it was most certainly a sharp change in man's relation to his Creator. He adopted toward God an altered attitude, and by so doing destroyed the proper Creator-creature relation in which, unknown to him, his true happiness lay. Essentially salvation is the restoration of a right relation between man and his Creator, a bringing back to normal of the Creator-creature relation.

A satisfactory spiritual life will begin with a complete change in relation between God and the sinner; not a judicial change merely, but a conscious and experienced change affecting the sinner's whole nature. The atonement in Jesus' blood makes such a change judicially possible and the working of the Holy Spirit makes it emotionally satisfying. The story of the prodigal son perfectly illustrates this latter phase. He had brought a world of trouble upon himself by forsaking the position which he had properly held as son of his father. At bottom his restoration was nothing more than a re-establishing of the father-son relation which had existed from his birth and had been altered temporarily by his act of sinful rebellion. This story overlooks the legal aspects of redemption, but it makes beautifully clear the experiential aspects of salvation.

In determining relationships we must begin somewhere. There must be somewhere a fixed center against which everything else is measured, where the law of relativity does not enter and we can say

"IS" and make no allowances. Such a center is God. When God would make His Name known to mankind He could find no better word than "I AM." When He speaks in the first person He says, "I AM"; when we speak of Him we say, "He is"; when we speak to Him we say, "Thou art." Everyone and everything else measures from that fixed point. "I am that I am," says God, "I change not."

As the sailor locates his position on the sea by "shooting" the sun, so we may get our moral bearings by looking at God. We must begin with God. We are right when and only when we stand in a right position relative to God, and we are wrong so far and so long as we stand in any other position.

Much of our difficulty as seeking Christians stems from our unwillingness to take God as He is and adjust our lives accordingly. We insist upon trying to modify Him and to bring Him nearer to our own image. The flesh whimpers against the rigor of God's inexorable sentence and begs like Agag for a little mercy, a little indulgence of its carnal ways. It is no use. We can get a right start only by accepting God as He is and learning to love Him for what He is. As we go on to know Him better we shall find it a source of unspeakable joy that God is just what He is. Some of the most rapturous moments we know will be those we spend in reverent admiration of the Godhead. In those holy moments the very thought of change in Him will be too painful to endure.

So let us begin with God. Back of all, above all, before all is God; first in sequential order, above in rank and station, exalted in dignity and honor. As the self-existent One He gave being to all things, and all things exist out of Him and for Him. "Thou art worthy, O Lord, to receive glory and honour and power: for thou hast created all things, and for thy pleasure they are and were created."

Every soul belongs to God and exists by His pleasure. God being Who and What He is, and we being who and what we are, the only thinkable relation between us is one of full lordship on His part and complete submission on ours. We owe Him every honor that it is in our power to give Him. Our everlasting grief lies in giving Him anything less.

The pursuit of God will embrace the labor of bringing our total personality into conformity to His. And this not judicially, but actually.

I do not here refer to the act of justification by faith in Christ. I speak of a voluntary exalting of God to His proper station over us and a willing surrender of our whole being to the place of worshipful submission which the Creator-creature circumstance makes proper.

The moment we make up our minds that we are going on with this determination to exalt God over all we step out of the world's parade. We shall find ourselves out of adjustment to the ways of the world, and increasingly so as we make progress in the holy way. We shall acquire a new viewpoint; a new and different psychology will be formed within us; a new power will begin to surprise us by its upsurgings and its outgoings.

Our break with the world will be the direct outcome of our changed relation to God. For the world of fallen men does not honor God. Millions call themselves by His Name, it is true, and pay some token respect to Him, but a simple test will show how little He is really honored among them. Let the average man be put to the proof on the question of who is *above*, and his true position will be exposed. Let him be forced into making a choice between God and money, between God and men, between God and personal ambition, God and self, God and human love, and God will take second place every time. Those other things will be exalted above. However the man may protest, the proof is in the choices he makes day after day throughout his life.

"Be thou exalted" is the language of victorious spiritual experience. It is a little key to unlock the door to great treasures of grace. It is central in the life of God in the soul. Let the seeking man reach a place where life and lips join to say continually "Be thou exalted," and a thousand minor problems will be solved at once. His Christian life ceases to be the complicated thing it had been before and becomes the very essence of simplicity. By the exercise of his will he has set his course, and on that course he will stay as if guided by an automatic pilot. If blown off course for a moment by some adverse wind he will surely return again as by a secret bent of the soul. The hidden motions of the Spirit are working in his favor, and "the stars in their courses" fight for him. He has met his life problem at its center, and everything else must follow along.

Let no one imagine that he will lose anything of human dignity by this voluntary sell-out of his all to his God. He does not by this degrade himself as a man; rather he finds his right place of high honor as one made in the image of his Creator. His deep disgrace lay in his moral derangement, his unnatural usurpation of the place of God. His honor will be proved by restoring again that stolen throne. In exalting God over all he finds his own highest honor upheld.

Anyone who might feel reluctant to surrender his will to the will of another should remember Jesus' words, "Whosoever committeth sin is the servant of sin." We must of necessity be servant to someone, either to God or to sin. The sinner prides himself on his independence, completely overlooking the fact that he is the weak slave of the sins that rule his members. The man who surrenders to Christ exchanges a cruel slave driver for a kind and gentle Master whose yoke is easy and whose burden is light.

Made as we were in the image of God we scarcely find it strange to take again our God as our All. God was our original habitat and our hearts cannot but feel at home when they enter again that ancient and beautiful abode.

I hope it is clear that there is a logic behind God's claim to pre-eminence. That place is His by every right in earth or heaven. While we take to ourselves the place that is His the whole course of our lives is out of joint. Nothing will or can restore order till our hearts make the great decision: God shall be exalted above.

"Them that honour me I will honour," said God once to a priest of Israel, and that ancient law of the Kingdom stands today unchanged by the passing of time or the changes of dispensation. The whole Bible and every page of history proclaim the perpetuation of that law. "If any man serve me, him will my Father honour," said our Lord Jesus, tying in the old with the new and revealing the essential unity of His ways with men.

Sometimes the best way to see a thing is to look at its opposite. Eli and his sons are placed in the priesthood with the stipulation that they honor God in their lives and ministrations. This they fail to do, and God sends Samuel to announce the consequences. Unknown to Eli this law of reciprocal honor has been all the while secretly working, and now the time has come for judgment to fall. Hophni and Phineas, the degenerate priests, fall in battle, the wife of Hophni dies in childbirth,

Israel flees before her enemies, the ark of God is captured by the Philistines and the old man Eli falls backward and dies of a broken neck. Thus stark utter tragedy followed upon Eli's failure to honor God.

Now set over against this almost any Bible character who honestly tried to glorify God in his earthly walk. See how God winked at weaknesses and overlooked failures as He poured upon His servants grace and blessing untold. Let it be Abraham, Jacob, David, Daniel, Elijah or whom you will; honor followed honor as harvest the seed. The man of God set his heart to exalt God above all; God accepted his intention as fact and acted accordingly. Not perfection, but holy intention made the difference.

In our Lord Jesus Christ this law was seen in simple perfection. In His lowly manhood He humbled Himself and gladly gave all glory to His Father in heaven. He sought not His own honor, but the honor of God who sent Him. "If I honour myself," He said on one occasion, "my honour is nothing; it is my Father that honoureth me." So far had the proud Pharisees departed from this law that they could not understand one who honored God at his own expense. "I honour my Father," said Jesus to them, "and ye do dishonour me."

Another saying of Jesus, and a most disturbing one, was put in the form of a question, "How can ye believe, which receive honour one of another, and seek not the honour that cometh from God alone?" If I understand this correctly Christ taught here the alarming doctrine that the desire for honor among men made belief impossible. Is this sin at the root of religious unbelief? Could it be that those "intellectual difficulties" which men blame for their inability to believe are but smoke screens to conceal the real cause that lies behind them? Was it this greedy desire for honor from man that made men into Pharisees and Pharisees into Deicides? Is this the secret back of religious self-righteousness and empty worship? I believe it may be. The whole course of the life is upset by failure to put God where He belongs. We exalt ourselves instead of God and the curse follows.

In our desire after God let us keep always in mind that God also hath desire, and His desire is toward the sons of men, and more particularly toward those sons of men who will make the once-for-all decision to exalt Him over all. Such as these are precious to God above all treasures of earth or sea. In them God finds a theater where He can display His exceeding kindness toward us in Christ Jesus. With them God can walk unhindered, toward them He can act like the God He is.

In speaking thus I have one fear; it is that I may convince the mind before God can win the heart. For this God-above-all position is one not easy to take. The mind may approve it while not having the consent of the will to put it into effect. While the imagination races ahead to honor God, the will may lag behind and the man never guess how divided his heart is. The whole man must make the decision before the heart can know any real satisfaction. God wants us all, and He will not rest till He gets us all. No part of the man will do.

Let us pray over this in detail, throwing ourselves at God's feet and meaning everything we say. No one who prays thus in sincerity need wait long for tokens of divine acceptance. God will unveil His glory before His servant's eyes, and He will place all His treasures at the disposal of such a one, for He knows that His honor is safe in such consecrated hands.

O God, be Thou exalted over my possessions. Nothing of earth's treasures shall seem dear unto me if only Thou art glorified in my life. Be Thou exalted over my friendships. I am determined that Thou shalt be above all, though I must stand deserted and alone in the midst of the earth. Be Thou exalted above my comforts. Though it mean the loss of bodily comforts and the carrying of heavy crosses I shall keep my vow made this day before Thee. Be Thou exalted over my reputation. Make me ambitious to please Thee even if as a result I must sink into obscurity and my name be forgotten as a dream. Rise, O Lord, into Thy proper place of honor, above my ambitions, above my likes and dislikes, above my family, my health and even my life itself. Let me decrease that Thou mayest increase, let me sink that Thou mayest rise above. Ride forth upon me as Thou didst ride into Jerusalem mounted upon the humble little beast, a colt, the foal of an ass, and let me hear the children cry to Thee, "Hosanna in the highest."

IX Meekness and Rest

> Blessed are the meek: for they shall inherit the earth.—*Matt. 5:5*

A fairly accurate description of the human race might be furnished one unacquainted with it by taking the Beatitudes, turning them wrong side out and saying, "Here is your human race." For the exact opposite of the virtues in the Beatitudes are the very qualities which distinguish human life and conduct.

In the world of men we find nothing approaching the virtues of which Jesus spoke in the opening words of the famous Sermon on the Mount. Instead of poverty of spirit we find the rankest kind of pride; instead of mourners we find pleasure seekers; instead of meekness, arrogance; instead of hunger after righteousness we hear men saying, "I am rich and increased with goods and have need of nothing"; instead of mercy we find cruelty; instead of purity of heart, corrupt imaginings; instead of peacemakers we find men quarrelsome and resentful; instead of rejoicing in mistreatment we find them fighting back with every weapon at their command.

Of this kind of moral stuff civilized society is composed. The atmosphere is charged with it; we breathe it with every breath and drink it with our mother's milk. Culture and education refine these things slightly but leave them basically untouched. A whole world of literature has been created to justify this kind of life as the only normal one. And this is the more to be wondered at seeing that these are the evils which make life the bitter struggle it is for all of us. All our heartaches and a great many of our physical ills spring directly out of our sins. Pride, arrogance, resentfulness, evil imaginings, malice, greed: these are the sources of more human pain than all the diseases that ever afflicted mortal flesh.

Into a world like this the sound of Jesus' words comes wonderful and strange, a visitation from above. It is well that He spoke, for no one else could have done it as well; and it is good that we listen. His words are the essence of truth. He is not offering an opinion; Jesus never uttered opinions. He never guessed; He knew, and He knows. His words are not as Solomon's were, the sum of sound wisdom or the results of keen observation. He spoke out of the fulness of His Godhead, and His words are very Truth itself. He is the only one who could say "blessed" with complete authority, for He is the Blessed One come from the world above to confer blessedness upon mankind. And His words were supported by deeds mightier than any performed on this earth by any other man. It is wisdom for us to listen.

As was often so with Jesus, He used this word "meek" in a brief crisp sentence, and not till some time later did He go on to explain it. In the same book of Matthew He tells us more about it and applies it to our lives. "Come unto me, all ye that labour and are heavy laden, and I will give you rest. Take my yoke upon you, and learn of me; for I am meek and lowly in heart: and ye shall find rest unto your souls. For my yoke is easy, and my burden is light." Here we have two things standing in contrast to each other, a burden and a rest. The burden is not a local one, peculiar to those first hearers, but one which is borne by the whole human race. It consists not of political oppression or poverty or hard work. It is far deeper than that. It is felt by the rich as well as the poor for it is something from which wealth and idleness can never deliver us.

The burden borne by mankind is a heavy and a crushing thing. The word Jesus used means a load carried or toil borne to the point of exhaustion. Rest is simply release from that burden. It is not something we do, it is what comes to us when we cease to do. His own meekness, that is the rest.

Let us examine our burden. It is altogether an interior one. It attacks the heart and the mind and reaches the body only from within. First, there is the burden of *pride*. The labor of self-love is a heavy one indeed. Think for yourself whether much of your sorrow has not arisen from someone speaking slightingly of you. As long as you set yourself up as a little god to which you must be loyal there will be those who will delight to offer affront to your idol. How then can you hope to have inward peace? The heart's fierce effort to protect itself from every slight, to shield its touchy honor from the bad opinion of friend and enemy, will never let the mind have rest. Continue this fight through the years and the burden will become intolerable. Yet the sons of earth are carrying this burden continually, challenging every word spoken against them, cringing under every criticism, smarting under each fancied slight, tossing sleepless if another is preferred before them.

Such a burden as this is not necessary to bear. Jesus calls us to His rest, and meekness is His method. The meek man cares not at all who is greater than he, for he has long ago decided that the esteem of the world is not worth the effort. He develops toward himself a kindly sense of humor and learns to say, "Oh, so you have been overlooked? They have placed someone else before you? They have whispered that you are pretty small stuff after all? And now you feel hurt because the world is saying about you the very things you have been saying about yourself? Only yesterday you were telling God that you were nothing, a mere worm of the dust. Where is your consistency? Come on, humble yourself, and cease to care what men think."

The meek man is not a human mouse afflicted with a sense of his own inferiority. Rather he may be in his moral life as bold as a lion and as strong as Samson; but he has stopped being fooled about himself. He has accepted God's estimate of his own life. He knows he is as weak and helpless as God has declared him to be, but paradoxically, he knows at the same time that he is in the sight of God of more importance than angels. In himself, nothing; in God, everything. That is his motto. He knows well that the world will never see him as God sees him and he has stopped caring. He rests perfectly content to allow God to place His own values. He will be patient to wait for the day when everything will get its own price tag and real worth will come into its own. Then the righteous shall shine forth in the Kingdom of their Father. He is willing to wait for that day.

In the meantime he will have attained a place of soul rest. As he walks on in meekness he will be happy to let God defend him. The old struggle to defend himself is over. He has found the peace which meekness brings.

Then also he will get deliverance from the burden of *pretense*. By this I mean not hypocrisy, but the common human desire to put the best foot forward and hide from the world our real inward poverty. For sin has played many evil tricks upon us, and one has been the infusing into us a false sense of shame. There is hardly a man or woman who dares to be just what he or she is without doctoring up the impression. The fear of being found out gnaws like rodents within their hearts. The man of culture is haunted by the fear that he will some day come upon a man more cultured than himself. The learned man fears to meet a man more learned than he. The rich man sweats under the fear that his clothes or his car or his house will sometime be made to look cheap by comparison with those of another rich man. So-called "society" runs by a motivation not higher than this, and the poorer classes on their level are little better.

Let no one smile this off. These burdens are real, and little by little they kill the victims of this evil and unnatural way of life. And the psychology created by years of this kind of thing makes true meekness seem as unreal as a dream, as aloof as a star. To all the victims of the gnawing disease Jesus says, "Ye must become as little children." For little children do not compare; they receive direct enjoyment from what they have without relating it to something else or someone else. Only as they get older and sin begins to stir within their hearts do jealousy and envy appear. Then they are unable to enjoy what they have if someone else has something larger or better. At that early age does the galling burden come down upon their tender souls, and it never leaves them till Jesus sets them free.

Another source of burden is *artificiality*. I am sure that most people live in secret fear that some day they will be careless and by chance an enemy or friend will be allowed to peep into their poor empty souls. So they are never relaxed. Bright people are tense and alert in fear that they may be trapped into saying something common or stupid. Traveled people are afraid that they may meet some Marco Polo who is able to describe some remote place where they have never been.

This unnatural condition is part of our sad heritage of sin, but in our day it is aggravated by our whole way of life. Advertising is largely based upon this habit of pretense. "Courses" are offered in this or that field of human learning frankly appealing to the victim's desire to shine at a party. Books are sold, clothes and cosmetics are peddled, by playing continually upon this desire to appear what we are not. Artificiality is one curse that will drop away the moment we kneel at Jesus' feet and surrender ourselves to His meekness. Then we will not care what people think of us so long as God is pleased. Then *what we are* will be everything; what we appear will take its place far down the scale of interest for us. Apart from sin we have nothing of which to be ashamed. Only an evil desire to shine makes us want to appear other than we are.

The heart of the world is breaking under this load of pride and pretense. There is no release from our burden apart from the meekness of Christ. Good keen reasoning may help slightly, but so strong is this vice that if we push it down one place it will come up somewhere else. To men and women everywhere Jesus says, "Come unto me, and I will give you rest." The rest He offers is the rest of meekness, the blessed relief which comes when we accept ourselves for what we are and cease to pretend. It will take some courage at first, but the needed grace will come as we learn that we are sharing this new and easy yoke with the strong Son of God Himself. He calls it "my yoke," and He walks at one end while we walk at the other.

Lord, make me childlike. Deliver me from the urge to compete with another for place or prestige or position. I would be simple and artless as a little child. Deliver me from pose and pretense. Forgive me for thinking of myself. Help me to forget myself and find my true peace in beholding Thee. That Thou mayest answer this prayer I humble myself before Thee. Lay upon me Thy easy yoke of self-forgetfulness that through it I may find rest. Amen.

X *The Sacrament of Living*

> Whether therefore ye eat, or drink, or whatsoever ye do, do all to the glory of God.—*I Cor. 10:31*

One of the greatest hindrances to internal peace which the Christian encounters is the common habit of dividing our lives into two areas, the sacred and the secular. As these areas are conceived to exist apart from each other and to be morally and spiritually incompatible, and as we are compelled by the necessities of living to be always crossing back and forth from the one to the other, our inner lives tend to break up so that we live a divided instead of a unified life.

Our trouble springs from the fact that we who follow Christ inhabit at once two worlds, the spiritual and the natural. As children of Adam we live our lives on earth subject to the limitations of the flesh and the weaknesses and ills to which human nature is heir. Merely to live among men requires of us years of hard toil and much care and attention to the things of this world. In sharp contrast to this is our life in the Spirit. There we enjoy another and higher kind of life; we are children of God; we possess heavenly status and enjoy intimate fellowship with Christ.

This tends to divide our total life into two departments. We come unconsciously to recognize two sets of actions. The first are performed with a feeling of satisfaction and a firm assurance that they are pleasing to God. These are the sacred acts and they are usually thought to be prayer, Bible reading, hymn singing, church attendance and such other acts as spring directly from faith. They may be known by the fact that they have no direct relation to this world, and would have no meaning whatever except as faith shows us another world, "an house not made with hands, eternal in the heavens."

Over against these sacred acts are the secular ones. They include all of the ordinary activities of life which we share with the sons and daughters of Adam: eating, sleeping, working, looking after the needs of the body and performing our dull and prosaic duties here on earth. These we often do reluctantly and with many misgivings, often apologizing to God for what we consider a waste of time and strength. The upshot of this is that we are uneasy most of the time. We go about our common tasks with a feeling of deep frustration, telling ourselves pensively that there's a better day coming when we shall slough off this earthly shell and be bothered no more with the affairs of this world.

This is the old sacred-secular antithesis. Most Christians are caught in its trap. They cannot get a satisfactory adjustment between the claims of the two worlds. They try to walk the tight rope between two kingdoms and they find no peace in either. Their strength is reduced, their outlook confused and their joy taken from them.

I believe this state of affairs to be wholly unnecessary. We have gotten ourselves on the horns of a dilemma, true enough, but the dilemma is not real. It is a creature of misunderstanding. The sacred-secular antithesis has no foundation in the New Testament. Without doubt a more perfect understanding of Christian truth will deliver us from it.

The Lord Jesus Christ Himself is our perfect example, and He knew no divided life. In the Presence of His Father He lived on earth without strain from babyhood to His death on the cross. God accepted the offering of His total life, and made no distinction between act and act. "I do always the things that please him," was His brief summary of His own life as it related to the Father. As He moved among men He was poised and restful. What pressure and suffering He endured grew out of His position as the world's sin bearer; they were never the result of moral uncertainty or spiritual maladjustment.

Paul's exhortation to "do all to the glory of God" is more than pious idealism. It is an integral part of the sacred revelation and is to be accepted as the very Word of Truth. It opens before us the possibility of making every act of our lives contribute to the glory of God. Lest we should be too timid to include everything, Paul mentions specifically eating and drinking. This humble privilege we share with the beasts that perish. If these lowly animal acts can be so performed as to honor God, then it becomes difficult to conceive of one that cannot.

That monkish hatred of the body which figures so prominently in the works of certain early devotional writers is wholly without support in the Word of God. Common modesty is found in the Sacred Scriptures, it is true, but never prudery or a false sense of shame. The New Testament accepts as a matter of course that in His incarnation our Lord took upon Him a real human body, and no effort is made to steer around the downright implications of such a fact. He lived in that body here among men and never once performed a non-sacred act. His presence in human flesh sweeps away forever the evil notion that there is about the human body something innately offensive to the Deity. God created our bodies, and we do not offend Him by placing the responsibility where it belongs. He is not ashamed of the work of His own hands.

Perversion, misuse and abuse of our human powers should give us cause enough to be ashamed. Bodily acts done in sin and contrary to nature can never honor God. Wherever the human will introduces moral evil we have no longer our innocent and harmless powers as God made them; we have instead an abused and twisted thing which can never bring glory to its Creator.

Let us, however, assume that perversion and abuse are not present. Let us think of a Christian believer in whose life the twin wonders of repentance and the new birth have been wrought. He is now living according to the will of God as he understands it from the written Word. Of such a one it may be said that every act of his life is or can be as truly sacred as prayer or baptism or the Lord's Supper. To say this is not to bring all acts down to one dead level; it is rather to lift every act up into a living kingdom and turn the whole life into a sacrament.

If a sacrament is an external expression of an inward grace than we need not hesitate to accept the above thesis. By one act of consecration of our total selves to God we can make every subsequent act express that consecration. We need no more be ashamed of our body—the fleshly servant that carries us through life—than Jesus was of the humble beast upon which He rode into Jerusalem. "The Lord hath need of him" may well apply to our mortal bodies. If Christ dwells in us we may bear about the Lord of glory as the little beast did of old and give occasion to the multitudes to cry, "Hosanna in the highest."

That we *see* this truth is not enough. If we would escape from the toils of the sacred-secular dilemma the truth must "run in our blood" and condition the complexion of our thoughts. We must practice living to the glory of God, actually and determinedly. By meditation upon this truth, by talking it over with God often in our prayers, by recalling it to our minds frequently as we move about among men, a *sense* of its wondrous meaning will begin to take hold of us. The old painful duality will go down before a restful unity of life. The knowledge that we are all God's, that He has received all and rejected nothing, will unify our inner lives and make everything sacred to us.

This is not quite all. Long-held habits do not die easily. It will take intelligent thought and a great deal of reverent prayer to escape completely from the sacred-secular psychology. For instance it may be difficult for the average Christian to get hold of the idea that his daily labors can be performed as acts of worship acceptable to God by Jesus Christ. The old antithesis will crop up in the back of his head sometimes to disturb his peace of mind. Nor will that old serpent the devil take all this lying down. He will be there in the cab or at the desk or in the field to remind the Christian that he is giving the better part of his day to the things of this world and allotting to his religious duties only a trifling portion of his time. And unless great care is taken this will create confusion and bring discouragement and heaviness of heart.

We can meet this successfully only by the exercise of an aggressive faith. We must offer all our acts to God and believe that He accepts them. Then hold firmly to that position and keep insisting that every act of every hour of the day and night be included in the transaction. Keep reminding God in our times of private prayer that we mean every act for His glory; then supplement those times by a thousand thought-prayers as we go about the job of living. Let us practice the fine art of making every work a priestly ministration. Let us believe that God is in all our simple deeds and learn to find Him there.

A concomitant of the error which we have been discussing is the sacred-secular antithesis as applied to places. It is little short of astonishing that we can read the New Testament and still believe in the inherent sacredness of places as distinguished from other places. This error is so widespread that one feels all alone when he tries to combat it. It has acted as a kind of dye to color the thinking of religious persons and has colored the eyes as well so that it is all but impossible to detect its fallacy. In the face of every New Testament teaching to the contrary it has been said and sung throughout the centuries and accepted as a part of the Christian message, the which it most surely is not. Only the Quakers, so far as my knowledge goes, have had the perception to see the error and the courage to expose it.

Here are the facts as I see them. For four hundred years Israel had dwelt in Egypt, surrounded by the crassest idolatry. By the hand of Moses they were brought out at last and started toward the land of promise. The very idea of holiness had been lost to them. To correct this, God began at the bottom. He localized Himself in the cloud and fire and later when the tabernacle had been built He dwelt in fiery manifestation in the Holy of Holies. By innumerable distinctions God taught Israel the difference between holy and unholy. There were holy days, holy vessels, holy garments. There were washings, sacrifices, offerings of many kinds. By these means Israel learned that *God is holy*. It was this that He was teaching them. Not the holiness of things or places, but the holiness of Jehovah was the lesson they must learn.

Then came the great day when Christ appeared. Immediately He began to say, "Ye have heard that it was said by them of old time—but *I* say unto you." The Old Testament schooling was over. When Christ died on the cross the veil of the temple was rent from top to bottom. The Holy of Holies was opened to everyone who would enter in faith. Christ's words were remembered, "The hour cometh, when ye shall neither in this mountain, nor yet at Jerusalem, worship the Father.... But the hour cometh, and now is, when the true worshippers shall worship the Father in spirit and in truth: for the Father seeketh such to worship Him. God is Spirit, and they that worship him must worship him in spirit and in truth."

Shortly after, Paul took up the cry of liberty and declared all meats clean, every day holy, all places sacred and every act acceptable to God. The sacredness of times and places, a half-light necessary to the education of the race, passed away before the full sun of spiritual worship.

The essential spirituality of worship remained the possession of the Church until it was slowly lost with the passing of the years. Then the natural *legality* of the fallen hearts of men began to introduce the old distinctions. The Church came to observe again days and seasons and times. Certain places were chosen and marked out as holy in a special sense. Differences were observed between one and another day or place or person, "The sacraments" were first two, then three, then four until with the triumph of Romanism they were fixed at seven.

In all charity, and with no desire to reflect unkindly upon any Christian, however misled, I would point out that the Roman Catholic church represents today the sacred-secular heresy carried to its logical conclusion. Its deadliest effect is the complete cleavage it introduces between religion and life. Its teachers attempt to avoid this snare by many footnotes and multitudinous explanations, but the mind's instinct for logic is too strong. In practical living the cleavage is a fact.

From this bondage reformers and puritans and mystics have labored to free us. Today the trend in conservative circles is back toward that bondage again. It is said that a horse after it has been led out of a burning building will sometimes by a strange obstinacy break loose from its rescuer and dash back into the building again to perish in the flame. By some such stubborn tendency toward error Fundamentalism in our day is moving back toward spiritual slavery. The observation of days and times is becoming more and more prominent among us. "Lent" and "holy week" and "good" Friday are words heard more and more frequently upon the lips of gospel Christians. We do not know when we are well off.

In order that I may be understood and not be misunderstood I would throw into relief the practical implications of the teaching for which I have been arguing, i.e., the sacramental quality of every day living. Over against its positive meanings I should like to point out a few things it does not mean.

It does not mean, for instance, that everything we do is of equal importance with everything else we do or may do. One act of a good man's life may differ widely from another in importance. Paul's sewing of tents was not equal to his writing of an Epistle to the Romans, but both were accepted of God and both were true acts of worship. Certainly it is more important to lead a soul to Christ than to plant a garden, but the planting of the garden *can* be as holy an act as the winning of a soul.

Again, it does not mean that every man is as useful as every other man. Gifts differ in the body of Christ. A Billy Bray is not to be compared with a Luther or a Wesley for sheer usefulness to the Church and to the world; but the service of the less gifted brother is as pure as that of the more gifted, and God accepts both with equal pleasure.

The "layman" need never think of his humbler task as being inferior to that of his minister. Let every man abide in the calling wherein he is called and his work will be as sacred as the work of the ministry. It is not what a man does that determines whether his work is sacred or secular, it is *why* he does it. The motive is everything. Let a man sanctify the Lord God in his heart and he can thereafter do no common act. All he does is good and acceptable to God through Jesus Christ. For such a man, living itself will be sacramental and the whole world a sanctuary. His entire life will be a priestly ministration. As he performs his never so simple task he will hear the voice of the seraphim saying, "Holy, Holy, Holy, is the Lord of hosts: the whole earth is full of his glory."

Lord, I would trust Thee completely; I would be altogether Thine; I would exalt Thee above all. I desire that I may feel no sense of possessing anything outside of Thee. I want constantly to be aware of Thy overshadowing Presence and to hear Thy speaking Voice. I long to live in restful sincerity of heart. I want to live so fully in the Spirit that all my thought may be as sweet incense ascending to Thee and every act of my life may be an act of worship. Therefore I pray in the words of Thy great servant of old, "I beseech Thee so for to cleanse the intent of mine heart with the unspeakable gift of Thy grace, that I may perfectly love Thee and worthily praise Thee." And all this I confidently believe Thou wilt grant me through the merits of Jesus Christ Thy Son. Amen.

Lord,
Teach Us To Pray

by

Andrew Murray

LORD, TEACH US TO PRAY
OR THE ONLY TEACHER.

The disciples had been with Christ, and seen Him pray. They had learnt to understand something of the connection between His wondrous life in public, and His secret life of prayer. They had learnt to believe in Him as a Master in the art of prayer—none could pray like Him. And so they came to Him with the request, 'Lord, teach us to pray.' And in after years they would have told us that there were few things more wonderful or blessed that He taught them than His lessons on prayer.

And now still it comes to pass, as He is praying in a certain place, that disciples who see Him thus engaged feel the need of repeating the same request, 'Lord, teach us to pray.' As we grow in the Christian life, the thought and the faith of the Beloved Master in His never-failing intercession becomes evermore precious, and the hope of being *Like Christ* in His intercession gains an attractiveness before unknown. And as we see Him pray, and remember that there is none who can pray like Him, and none who can teach like Him, we feel the petition of the disciples, 'Lord, teach us to pray,' is just what we need. And as we think how all He is and has, how He Himself is our very own, how He is Himself our life, we feel assured that we have but to ask, and He will be delighted to take us up into closer fellowship with Himself, and teach us to pray even as He prays.

Come, my brothers! Shall we not go to the Blessed Master and ask Him to enrol our names too anew in that school which He always keeps open for those who long to continue their studies in the Divine art of prayer and intercession? Yes, let us this very day say to the Master, as they did of old, 'Lord, teach us to pray.' As we meditate we shall find each word of the petition we bring to be full of meaning.

'Lord, teach us *to pray*.' Yes, *to pray*. This is what we need to be taught. Though in its beginnings prayer is so simple that the feeble child can pray, yet it is at the same time the highest and holiest work to which man can rise. It is fellowship with the Unseen and Most Holy One. The powers of the eternal world have been placed at its disposal. It is the very essence of true religion, the channel of all blessings, the secret of power and life. Not only for ourselves, but for others, for the Church, for the world, it is to prayer that God has given the right to take hold of Him and His strength. It is on prayer that the promises wait for their fulfilment, the kingdom for its coming, the glory of God for its full revelation. And for this blessed work, how slothful and unfit we are. It is only the Spirit of God can enable us to do it aright. How speedily we are deceived into a resting in the form, while the power is wanting. Our early training, the teaching of the Church, the influence of habit, the stirring of the emotions—how easily these lead to prayer which has no spiritual power, and avails but little. True prayer, that takes hold of God's strength, that availeth much, to which the gates of heaven are really opened wide—who would not cry, Oh for some one to teach me thus to pray?

Jesus has opened a school, in which He trains His redeemed ones, who specially desire it, to have power in prayer. Shall we not enter it with the petition, Lord! it is just this we need to be taught! O teach us to *pray*.

'Lord, teach *us* to pray.' Yes, *us*, Lord. We have read in Thy Word with what power Thy believing people of old used to pray, and what mighty wonders were done in answer to their prayers. And if this took place under the Old Covenant, in the time of preparation, how much more wilt Thou not now, in these days of fulfilment, give Thy people this sure sign of Thy presence in their midst. We have heard the promises given to Thine apostles of the power of prayer in Thy name, and have seen how gloriously they experienced their truth: we know for certain, they can become true to us too. We hear continually even in these days what glorious tokens of Thy power Thou dost still give to those who trust Thee fully. Lord! these all are men of like passions with ourselves; teach *us* to pray so too. The promises are for us, the powers and gifts of the heavenly world are for us. O teach *us* to pray so that we may receive abundantly. To us too Thou hast entrusted Thy work, on our prayer too the coming of Thy kingdom depends, in our prayer too Thou canst glorify Thy name; 'Lord, teach us to pray.' Yes, us, Lord; we offer ourselves as learners; we would indeed be taught of Thee. 'Lord, teach *us* to pray.'

'Lord, *teach* us to pray.' Yes, we feel the need now of being *taught* to pray. At first there is no work appears so simple; later on, none that is more difficult; and the confession is forced from us: We know not how to pray as we ought. It is true we have God's Word, with its clear and sure promises; but sin has so darkened our mind, that we know not always how to apply the Word. In spiritual things we do not always seek the most needful things, or fail in praying according to the law of the sanctuary. In temporal things we are still less able to avail ourselves of the wonderful liberty our Father has given us to ask what we need. And even when we know what to ask, how much there is still needed to make prayer acceptable. It must be to the glory of God, in full surrender to His will, in full assurance of faith, in the name of Jesus, and with a perseverance that, if need be, refuses to be denied. All this must be learned. It can only be learned in the school of much prayer, for practice makes perfect. Amid the painful consciousness of ignorance and unworthiness, in the struggle between believing and doubting, the heavenly art of effectual prayer is learnt. Because, even when we do not remember it, there is One, the Beginner and Finisher of faith and prayer, who watches over our praying, and sees to it that *in all who trust Him for it* their education in the school of prayer shall be carried on to perfection. Let but the deep undertone of all our prayer be the teachableness that comes from a sense of ignorance, and from faith in Him as a perfect teacher, and we may be sure we shall be taught, we shall learn to pray in power. Yes, we may depend upon it, He *teaches* to pray.

'*Lord*, teach us to pray.' None can teach like Jesus, none but Jesus; therefore we call on Him, 'Lord, teach us to pray.' A pupil needs a teacher, who knows his work, who has the gift of teaching, who in patience and love will descend to the pupil's needs. Blessed be God! Jesus is all this and much more. He knows what prayer is. It is Jesus, praying Himself, who teaches to pray. He knows what prayer is. He learned it amid the trials and tears of His earthly life. In heaven it is still His beloved work: His life there is prayer. Nothing delights Him more than to find those whom He can take with Him into the Father's presence, whom He can clothe with power to pray down God's blessing on those around them, whom He can train to be His fellow-workers in the intercession by which the kingdom is to be revealed on earth. He knows how to teach. Now by the urgency of felt need, then by the confidence with which joy inspires. Here by the teaching of the Word, there by the testimony of another believer who knows what it is to have prayer heard. By His Holy Spirit, He has access to our heart, and teaches us to pray by showing us the sin that hinders the prayer, or giving us the assurance that we please God. He teaches, by giving not only thoughts of what to ask or how to ask, but by breathing within us the very spirit of prayer, by living within us as the Great Intercessor. We may indeed and most joyfully say, 'Who teacheth like Him?' Jesus never taught His disciples how to preach, only how to pray. He did not speak much of what was needed to preach well, but much of praying well. To know how to speak to God is more than knowing how to speak to man. Not power with men, but power with God is the first thing. Jesus loves to teach us how to pray.

What think you, my beloved fellow-disciples! would it not be just what we need, to ask the Master for a month to give us a course of special lessons on the art of prayer? As we meditate on the words He spake on earth, let us yield ourselves to His teaching in the fullest confidence that, with such a teacher, we shall make progress. Let us take time not only to meditate, but to pray, to tarry at the foot of the throne, and be trained to the work of intercession. Let us do so in the assurance that amidst our stammerings and fears He is carrying on His work most beautifully. He will breathe His own life, which is all prayer, into us. As He makes us partakers of His righteousness and His life, He will of His intercession too. As the members of His body, as a holy priesthood, we shall take part in His priestly work of pleading and prevailing with God for men. Yes, let us most joyfully say, ignorant and feeble though we be, 'Lord, teach us to pray.'

'Lord, Teach Us To Pray.'

Blessed Lord! who ever livest to pray, Thou canst teach me too to pray, me to live ever to pray. In this Thou lovest to make me share Thy glory in heaven, that I should pray without ceasing, and ever stand as a priest in the presence of my God.

Lord Jesus! I ask Thee this day to enrol my name among those who confess that they know not how to pray as they ought, and especially ask Thee for a course of teaching in prayer. Lord! teach me to tarry with Thee in the school, and give Thee time to train me. May a deep sense of my ignorance, of the wonderful privilege and power of prayer, of the need of the Holy Spirit as the Spirit of prayer, lead me to cast away my thoughts of what I think I know, and make me kneel before Thee in true teachableness and poverty of spirit.

And fill me, Lord, with the confidence that with such a teacher as Thou art I shall learn to pray. In the assurance that I have as my teacher, Jesus, who is ever praying to the Father, and by His prayer rules the destinies of His Church and the world, I will not be afraid. As much as I need to know of the mysteries of the prayer-world, Thou wilt unfold for me. And when I may not know, Thou wilt teach me to be strong in faith, giving glory to God.

Blessed Lord! Thou wilt not put to shame Thy scholar who trusts Thee, nor, by Thy grace, would he Thee either. Amen.

'IN SPIRIT AND TRUTH;
OR THE TRUE WORSHIPPERS.

'The hour cometh, and now is, when the true worshippers shall worship the Father in spirit and truth: for such doth the Father seek to be His worshippers. God is a Spirit: and they that worship Him must worship Him in spirit and truth.'—John iv. 23, 24.

These words of Jesus to the woman of Samaria are His first recorded teaching on the subject of prayer. They give us some wonderful first glimpses into the world of prayer. The Father *seeks* worshippers: our worship satisfies His loving heart and is a joy to Him. He seeks *true worshippers*, but finds many not such as He would have them. True worship is that which is *in spirit and truth*. *The Son has come* to open the way for this worship in spirit and in truth, and teach it us. And so one of our first lessons in the school of prayer must be to understand what it is to pray in spirit and in truth, and to know how we can attain to it.

To the woman of Samaria our Lord spoke of a threefold worship. There is, first, the ignorant worship of the Samaritans: 'Ye worship that which ye know not.' The second, the intelligent worship of the Jew, having the true knowledge of God: 'We worship that which we know; for salvation is of the Jews.' And then the new, the spiritual worship which He Himself has come to introduce: 'The hour is coming, and is now, when the true worshippers shall worship the Father in spirit and truth.' From the connection it is evident that the words 'in spirit and truth' do not mean, as is often thought, earnestly, from the heart, in sincerity. The Samaritans had the five books of Moses and some knowledge of God; there was doubtless more than one among them who honestly and earnestly sought God in prayer. The Jews had the true full revelation of

God in His word, as thus far given; there were among them godly men, who called upon God with their whole heart. And yet not 'in spirit and truth,' in the full meaning of the words. Jesus says, '*The hour is coming, and now is:*' it is only in and through Him that the worship of God will be in spirit and truth.

Among Christians one still finds the three classes of worshippers. Some who in their ignorance hardly know what they ask: they pray earnestly, and yet receive but little. Others there are, who have more correct knowledge, who try to pray with all their mind and heart, and often pray most earnestly, and yet do not attain to the full blessedness of worship in spirit and truth. It is into this third class we must ask our Lord Jesus to take us; we must be taught of Him how to worship in spirit and truth. This alone is spiritual worship; this makes us worshippers such as the Father seeks. In prayer everything will depend on our understanding well and practising the worship in spirit and truth.

'God is *a Spirit* and they that worship Him must worship Him *in spirit* and truth.' The first thought suggested here by the Master is that there must be harmony between God and His worshippers; such as God is, must His worship be. This is according to a principle which prevails throughout the universe: we look for correspondence between an object and the organ to which it reveals or yields itself. The eye has an inner fitness for the light, the ear for sound. The man who would truly worship God, would find and know and possess and enjoy God, must be in harmony with Him, must have a capacity for receiving Him. Because God *is Spirit*, we must worship *in spirit*. As God is, so His worshipper.

And what does this mean? The woman had asked our Lord whether Samaria or Jerusalem was the true place of worship. He answers that henceforth worship is no longer to be limited to a certain place: 'Woman, believe Me, *the hour cometh* when neither in this mountain, nor in Jerusalem, shall ye worship the Father.' As God is Spirit, not bound by space or time, but in His infinite perfection always and everywhere the same, so His worship would henceforth no longer be confined by place or form, but spiritual as God Himself is spiritual. A lesson of deep importance. How much our Christianity suffers from this, that it is confined to certain times and places. A man who seeks to pray earnestly in the church or in the closet, spends the greater part of the week or the day in a spirit entirely at variance with that in which he prayed. His worship was the work of a fixed place or hour, not of his whole being. God is a spirit: He is the Everlasting and Unchangeable One; what He is, He is always and in truth. Our worship must even so be in spirit and truth: His worship must be the spirit of our life; our life must be worship in spirit as God is Spirit.

'God is a Spirit: and they that worship Him must worship Him in spirit and truth.' The second thought that comes to us is that this worship in the spirit must come from God Himself. God is Spirit: He alone has Spirit to give. It was for this He sent His Son, to fit us for such spiritual worship, by giving us the Holy Spirit. It is of His own work that Jesus speaks when He says twice, 'The hour cometh,' and then adds, 'and is now.' He came to baptize with the Holy Spirit; the Spirit could not stream forth till He was glorified (*John i. 33, vii. 37, 38, xvi. 7*). It was when He had made an end of sin, and entering into the Holiest of all with His blood, had there on our behalf *received* the Holy Spirit (*Acts ii. 33*), that He could send Him down to us as the Spirit of the Father. It was when Christ had redeemed us, and we in Him had received the position of children, that the Father sent forth the Spirit of His Son into our hearts to cry, 'Abba, Father.' The worship in spirit is the worship of the Father in the Spirit of Christ, the Spirit of Sonship.

This is the reason why Jesus here uses the name of Father. We never find one of the Old Testament saints personally appropriate the name of child or call God his Father. The worship *of the Father* is only possible to those to whom the Spirit of the Son has been given. The worship *in spirit* is only possible to those to whom the Son has revealed the Father, and who have received the spirit of Sonship. It is only Christ who opens the way and teaches the worship in spirit.

And *in truth*. That does not only mean, *in sincerity*. Nor does it only signify, in accordance with the truth of God's Word. The expression is one of deep and Divine meaning. Jesus is 'the only-begotten of the Father, *full of* grace and *truth*.' 'The law was given by Moses; grace and *truth came* by Jesus Christ.' Jesus says, '*I am the truth* and the life.' In the Old Testament all was shadow and promise; Jesus brought and gives the reality, *the substance*, of things hoped for. In Him the blessings and powers of the eternal life are our actual possession and experience. Jesus is full of grace and truth; the Holy Spirit is the Spirit of truth;

through Him the grace that is in Jesus is ours indeed, and truth a positive communication out of the Divine life. And so worship in spirit is worship *in truth*; actual living fellowship with God, a real correspondence and harmony between the Father, who is a Spirit, and the child praying in the spirit.

What Jesus said to the woman of Samaria, she could not at once understand. Pentecost was needed to reveal its full meaning. We are hardly prepared at our first entrance into the school of prayer to grasp such teaching. We shall understand it better later on. Let us only begin and take the lesson as He gives it. We are carnal and cannot bring God the worship He seeks. But Jesus came to give the Spirit: He has given Him to us. Let the disposition in which we set ourselves to pray be what Christ's words have taught us. Let there be the deep confession of our inability to bring God the worship that is pleasing to Him; the childlike teachableness that waits on Him to instruct us; the simple faith that yields itself to the breathing of the Spirit. Above all, let us hold fast the blessed truth—we shall find that the Lord has more to say to us about it—that the knowledge of the Fatherhood of God, the revelation of His infinite Fatherliness in our hearts, the faith in the infinite love that gives us His Son and His Spirit to make us children, is indeed the secret of prayer in spirit and truth. This is the new and living way Christ opened up for us. To have Christ the Son, and *The Spirit of the Son*, dwelling within us, and revealing the Father, this makes us true, spiritual worshippers.

'Lord, Teach Us To Pray.'

Blessed Lord! I adore the love with which Thou didst teach a woman, who had refused Thee a cup of water, what the worship of God must be. I rejoice in the assurance that Thou wilt no less now instruct Thy disciple, who comes to Thee with a heart that longs to pray in spirit and in truth. O my Holy Master! do teach me this blessed secret.

Teach me that the worship in spirit and truth is not of man, but only comes from Thee; that it is not only a thing of times and seasons, but the outflowing of a life in Thee. Teach me to draw near to God in prayer under the deep impression of my ignorance and my having nothing in myself to offer Him, and at the same time of the provision Thou, my

Saviour, makest for the Spirit's breathing in my childlike stammerings. I do bless Thee that in Thee I am a child, and have a child's liberty of access; that in Thee I have the spirit of Sonship and of worship of truth. Teach me, above all, Blessed Son of the Father, how it is the revelation of the Father that gives confidence in prayer; and let the infinite Fatherliness of God's Heart be my joy and strength for a life of prayer and of worship. Amen.

PRAY TO THY FATHER WHICH IS IN SECRET
OR ALONE WITH GOD.

'But thou, when thou prayest, enter into thine inner chamber, and having shut thy door, pray to thy Father which is in secret, and thy Father which seeth in secret shall recompense thee.'—Matt. vi. 6.

After Jesus had called His first disciples He gave them their first public teaching in the Sermon on the Mount. He there expounded to them the kingdom of God, its laws and its life. In that kingdom God is not only King, but Father; He not only gives all, but is Himself all. In the knowledge and fellowship of Him alone is its blessedness. Hence it came as a matter of course that the revelation of prayer and the prayer-life was a part of His teaching concerning the New Kingdom He came to set up. Moses gave neither command nor regulation with regard to prayer: even the prophets say little directly of the duty of prayer; it is Christ who teaches to pray.

And the first thing the Lord teaches His disciples is that they must have a secret place for prayer; every one must have some solitary spot where he can be alone with his God. Every teacher must have a schoolroom. We have learnt to know and accept Jesus as our only teacher in the school of prayer. He has already taught us at Samaria that worship is no longer confined to times and places; that worship, spiritual true worship, is a thing of the spirit and the life; the whole man must in his whole life be worship in spirit and truth. And yet He wants each one to choose for himself the fixed spot where He can daily meet him. That inner chamber, that solitary place, is Jesus' schoolroom. That spot may be anywhere; that spot may change from day to day if we have to change our abode; but that secret place there must be, with the quiet time in which the pupil places himself in the Master's presence, to be by Him prepared to worship the Father. There alone, but there most surely, Jesus comes to us to teach us to pray.

A teacher is always anxious that his schoolroom should be bright and attractive, filled with the light and air of heaven, a place where pupils long to come, and love to stay. In His first words on prayer in the Sermon on the Mount, Jesus seeks to set the inner chamber before us in its most attractive light. If we listen carefully, we soon notice what the chief thing is He has to tell us of our tarrying there. Three times He uses the name of Father: 'Pray to *thy Father*;' '*Thy Father* shall recompense thee;' *Your Father* knoweth what things ye have need of.' The first thing in closet-prayer is: I must meet my Father. The light that shines in the closet must be: the light of the Father's countenance. The fresh air from heaven with which Jesus would have filled the atmosphere in which I am to breathe and pray, is: God's Father-love, God's infinite Fatherliness. Thus each thought or petition we breathe out will be simple, hearty, childlike trust in the Father. This is how the Master teaches us to pray: He brings us into the Father's living presence. What we pray there must avail. Let us listen carefully to hear what the Lord has to say to us.

First, '*Pray to thy Father which is in secret.*' God is a God who hides Himself to the carnal eye. As long as in our worship of God we are chiefly occupied with our own thoughts and exercises, we shall not meet Him who is a Spirit, the unseen One. But to the man who withdraws himself from all that is of the world and man, and prepares to wait upon God alone, the Father will reveal Himself. As he forsakes and gives up and shuts out the world, and the life of the world, and surrenders himself to be led of Christ into the secret of God's presence, the light of the Father's love will rise upon him. The secrecy of the inner chamber and the closed door, the entire separation from all around us, is an image of, and so a help to, that inner spiritual sanctuary, the secret of God's tabernacle, within the veil, where our spirit truly comes into contact with the Invisible One. And so we are taught, at the very outset of our search after the secret of effectual prayer, to remember that it is in the inner chamber, where we are alone with the Father, that we shall learn to pray aright. The Father is in secret: in these words Jesus teaches us where He is waiting us, where He is always to be found. Christians often complain that private prayer is not what it should be. They feel weak and sinful, the heart is cold and dark; it is as if they have so little to pray, and in that little no faith or joy. They are discouraged and kept from prayer by the thought that they cannot come to the Father as they ought or as they wish. Child of God! listen to your Teacher. He tells you that when you go to private prayer your first thought must be: The Father is in secret, the Father waits me there. Just because your heart is cold and prayerless, get you into the presence of the loving Father. As a father pitieth his children, so the Lord pitieth you. Do not be thinking of how little you have to bring God, but of how much He wants to give you. Just place yourself before, and look up into, His face; think of His love, His wonderful, tender, pitying love. Just tell Him how sinful and cold and dark all is: it is the Father's loving heart will give light and warmth to yours. O do what Jesus says: Just shut the door, and pray to thy Father, which is in secret. Is it not wonderful? to be able to go alone with God, the infinite God. And then to look up and say: My Father!

'*And thy Father, which seeth in secret, will recompense thee.*' Here Jesus assures us that secret prayer cannot be fruitless: its blessing will show itself in our life. We have but in secret, alone with God, to entrust our life before men to Him; He will reward us openly; He will see to it that the answer to prayer be made manifest in His blessing upon us. Our Lord would thus teach us that as infinite Fatherliness and Faithfulness is that with which God meets us in secret, so on our part there should be the childlike simplicity of faith, the confidence that our prayer does bring down a blessing. 'He that cometh to God must believe that *He is a rewarder* of them that seek Him.' Not on the strong or the fervent feeling with which I pray does the blessing of the closet depend, but upon the love and the power of the Father to whom I there entrust my needs. And therefore the Master has but one desire: Remember your Father is, and sees and hears in secret; go there and stay there, and go again from there in the confidence: He will recompense. Trust Him for it; depend upon Him: prayer to the Father cannot be vain; He will reward you openly.

Still further to confirm this faith in the Father-love of God, Christ speaks a third word: '*Your Father knoweth what things ye have need of before ye ask Him.*' At first sight it might appear as if this thought made prayer less needful: God knows far better than we what we need. But as we get a deeper insight into what prayer really is, this truth will help much to strengthen our faith. It will teach us that we do not need, as the heathen, with the multitude and urgency of our words, to compel an unwilling God to listen to us. It will lead to a holy thoughtfulness and silence in prayer as it suggests the question: Does my Father really know that I need this? It will, when once we have been led by the Spirit to the certainty that our request is indeed something that, according to the Word, we do need for God's glory, give us wonderful confidence to say, My Father knows I need it and must have it. And if there be any delay in the answer, it will teach us in quiet perseverance to hold on: Father! Thou knowest I need it. O the blessed liberty and simplicity of a child that Christ our Teacher would fain cultivate in us, as we draw near to God: let us look up to the Father until His Spirit works it in us. Let us sometimes in our prayers, when we are in danger of being so occupied with our fervent, urgent petitions, as to forget that the Father knows and hears, let us hold still and just quietly say: My Father sees, my Father hears, my Father knows; it will help our faith to take the answer, and to say: We know that we have the petitions we have asked of Him.

And now, all ye who have anew entered the school of Christ to be taught to pray, take these lessons, practise them, and trust Him to perfect you in them. Dwell much in the inner chamber, with the door shut—shut in from men, shut up with God; it is there the Father waits you, it is there Jesus will teach you to pray. To be alone in secret with the Father: this be your highest joy. To be assured that the Father will openly reward the secret prayer, so that it cannot remain unblessed: this be your strength day by day. And to know that the Father knows that you need what you ask, this be your liberty to bring every need, in the assurance that your God will supply it according to His riches in glory in Christ Jesus.

'Lord, teach us to pray.'

Blessed Saviour! with my whole heart I do bless Thee for the appointment of the inner chamber, as the school where Thou meetest each of Thy pupils alone, and revealest to him the Father. O my Lord! strengthen my faith so in the Father's tender love and kindness, that as often as I feel sinful or troubled, the first instinctive thought may be to go where I know the Father waits me, and where prayer never can go unblessed. Let the thought that He knows my need before I ask, bring me, in great restfulness of faith, to trust that He will give what His child requires. O let the place of secret prayer become to me the most beloved spot on earth.

And, Lord! hear me as I pray that Thou wouldest everywhere bless the closets of Thy believing people. Let Thy wonderful revelation of a Father's tenderness free all young Christians from every thought of secret prayer as a duty or a burden, and lead them to regard it as the highest privilege of their life, a joy and a blessing. Bring back all who are discouraged, because they cannot find aught to bring Thee in prayer. O give them to understand that they have only to come with their emptiness to Him who has all to give, and delights to do it. Not, what they have to bring the Father, but what the Father waits to give them, be their one thought.

And bless especially the inner chamber of all Thy servants who are working for Thee, as the place where God's truth and God's grace is revealed to them, where they are daily anointed with fresh oil, where their strength is renewed, and the blessings are received in faith, with which they are to bless their fellow-men. Lord, draw us all in the closet nearer to Thyself and the Father. Amen.

'AFTER THIS MANNER PRAY;'
OR THE MODEL PRAYER.

> 'After this manner therefore pray ye: Our Father which art in heaven.'—Matt. vi. 9.

Every teacher knows the power of example. He not only tells the child what to do and how to do it, but shows him how it really can be done. In condescension to our weakness, our Heavenly Teacher has given us the very words we are to take with us as we draw near to our Father. We have in them a form of prayer in which there breathe the freshness and fulness of the Eternal Life. So simple that the child can lisp it, so divinely rich that it comprehends all that God can give. A form of prayer that becomes the model and inspiration for all other prayer, and yet always draws us back to itself as the deepest utterance of our souls before our God.

'*Our Father which art in heaven!*' To appreciate this word of adoration aright, I must remember that none of the saints had in Scripture ever ventured to address God as their Father. The invocation places us at once in the centre of the wonderful revelation the Son came to make of His Father as our Father too. It comprehends the mystery of redemption—Christ delivering us from the curse that we might become the children of God. The mystery of regeneration—the Spirit in the new birth giving us the new life. And the mystery of faith—ere yet the redemption is accomplished or understood, the word is given on the lips of the disciples to prepare them for the blessed experience still to come. The words are the key to the whole prayer, to all prayer. It takes time, it takes life to study them; it will take eternity to understand them fully. The knowledge of God's Father-love is the first and simplest, but also the last and highest lesson in the school of prayer. It is in the personal relation to the living God, and the personal conscious fellowship of love with Himself, that prayer begins. It is in the knowledge of God's Fatherliness, revealed by the Holy Spirit, that the power of prayer will be found to root and grow. In the infinite tenderness and pity and patience of the infinite Father, in His loving readiness to hear and to help, the life of prayer has its joy. O let us take time, until the Spirit has made these words to us spirit and truth, filling heart and life: 'Our Father which art in heaven.' Then we are indeed within the veil, in the secret place of power where prayer always prevails.

'*Hallowed be Thy name.*' There is something here that strikes us at once. While we ordinarily first bring our own needs to God in prayer, and then think of what belongs to God and His interests, the Master reverses the order. First, *Thy* name, *Thy* kingdom, *Thy* will; then, give *us*, forgive *us*, lead *us*, deliver *us*. The lesson is of more importance than we think. In true worship the Father must be first, must be all. The sooner I learn to forget myself in the desire that He may be glorified, the richer will the blessing be that prayer will bring to myself. No one ever loses by what he sacrifices for the Father.

This must influence all our prayer. There are two sorts of prayer: personal and intercessory. The latter ordinarily occupies the lesser part of our time and energy. This may not be. Christ has opened the school of prayer specially to train intercessors for the great work of bringing down, by their faith and prayer, the blessings of His work and love on the world around. There can be no deep growth in prayer unless this be made our aim. The little child may ask of the father only what it needs for itself; and yet it soon learns to say, Give some for sister too. But the grown-up son, who only lives for the father's interest and takes charge of the father's business, asks more largely, and gets all that is asked. And Jesus would train us to the blessed life of consecration and service, in which our interests are all subordinate to the Name, and the Kingdom, and the Will of the Father. O let us live for this, and let, on each act of adoration, Our Father! there follow in the same breath, *Thy* Name, *Thy* Kingdom, *Thy* Will;—for this we look up and long.

'*Hallowed be Thy name.*' What name? This new name of Father. The word *Holy* is the central word of the Old Testament; the *name* Father of the New. In this name of Love all the holiness and glory of God are now to be revealed. And how is the name to be hallowed? By God Himself: '*I will hallow* My great name which ye have profaned.' Our prayer must be that in ourselves, in all God's children, in presence of the world, God Himself would reveal the holiness, the Divine power, the hidden glory of the name of Father. The Spirit of the Father is the *Holy* Spirit: it is only when we yield ourselves to be led *of Him*, that the name will be *hallowed* in our prayer and our lives. Let us learn the prayer: 'Our Father, hallowed be Thy name.'

'*Thy kingdom come.*' The Father is a King and has a kingdom. The son and heir of a king has no higher ambition than the glory of his father's kingdom. In time of war or danger this becomes his passion; he can think of nothing else. The children of the Father are here in the enemy's territory, where the kingdom, which is in heaven, is not yet fully manifested. What more natural than that, when they learn to hallow the Father-name, they should long and cry with deep enthusiasm: 'Thy kingdom come.' The coming of the kingdom is the one great event on which the revelation of the Father's glory, the blessedness of His children, the salvation of the world depends. On our prayers too the coming of the kingdom waits. Shall we not join in the deep longing cry of the redeemed: 'Thy kingdom come'? Let us learn it in the school of Jesus.

'*Thy will be done, as in heaven, so on earth.*' This petition is too frequently applied alone to the *suffering* of the will of God. In heaven God's will is *done*, and the Master teaches the child to ask that the will may be done on earth just as in heaven: in the spirit of adoring submission and ready obedience. Because the will of God is the glory of heaven, the doing of it is the blessedness of heaven. As the will is done, the kingdom of heaven comes into the heart. And wherever faith has accepted the Father's love, obedience accepts the Father's will. The surrender to, and the prayer for a life of heaven-like obedience, is the spirit of childlike prayer.

'*Give us this day our daily bread.*' When first the child has yielded himself to the Father in the care for His Name, His Kingdom, and His Will, he has full liberty to ask for his daily bread. A master cares for the food of his servant, a general of his soldiers, a father of his child. And will not the Father in heaven care for the child who has in prayer given himself up to His interests? We may indeed in full confidence say: Father, I live for Thy honor and Thy work; I know Thou carest for me. Consecration to God and His will gives wonderful liberty in prayer for temporal things: the whole earthly life is given to the Father's loving care.

'*And forgive us our debts as we also have forgiven our debtors.*' As bread is the first need of the body, so forgiveness for the soul. And the provision for the one is as sure as for the other. We are children, but sinners too; our right of access to the Father's presence we owe to the precious blood and the forgiveness it has won for us. Let us beware of the prayer for forgiveness becoming a formality: only what is really confessed is really forgiven. Let us in faith accept the forgiveness as promised: as a spiritual reality, an actual transaction between God and us, it is the entrance into all the Father's love and all the privileges of children. Such forgiveness, as a living experience, is impossible without a forgiving spirit to others: as *forgiven* expresses the heavenward, so *forgiving* the earthward, relation of God's child. In each prayer to the Father I must be able to say that I know of no one whom I do not heartily love.

'*And lead us not into temptation, but deliver us from the evil one.*' Our daily bread, the pardon of our sins, and then our being kept from all sin and the power of the evil one, in these three petitions all our personal need is comprehended. The prayer for bread and pardon must be accompanied by the surrender to live in all things in holy obedience to the Father's will, and the believing prayer in everything to be kept by the power of the indwelling Spirit from the power of the evil one.

Children of God! it is thus Jesus would have us to pray to the Father in heaven. O let His Name, and Kingdom, and Will, have the first place in our love; His providing, and pardoning, and keeping love will be our sure portion. So the prayer will lead us up to the true child-life: the Father all to the child, the Father all for the child. We shall understand how Father and child, the *Thine* and the *Our*, are all one, and how the heart that begins its prayer with the God-devoted Thine, will have the power in faith to speak out the Our too. Such prayer will, indeed, be the fellowship and interchange of love, always bringing us back in trust and worship to Him who is not only the Beginning but the End: 'For thine is the kingdom, and the power, and the glory, for ever, Amen.' Son of the Father, teach us to pray, 'Our Father.'

'Lord, teach us to pray.'

O Thou who art the only-begotten Son, teach us, we beseech Thee, to pray, 'Our Father.' We thank Thee, Lord, for these Living Blessed Words which Thou hast given us. We thank Thee for the millions who in them have learnt to know and worship the Father, and for what they have been to us. Lord! it is as if we needed days and weeks in Thy school with each separate petition; so deep and full are they. But we look to Thee to lead us deeper into their meaning: do it, we pray Thee, for Thy Name's sake; Thy name is Son of the Father.

Lord! Thou didst once say: 'No man knoweth the Father save the Son, and he to whom the Son willeth to reveal Him.' And again: 'I made known unto them Thy name, and will make it known, that the love wherewith Thou hast loved Me may be in them.' Lord Jesus! reveal to us the Father. Let His name, His infinite Father-love, the love with which He loved Thee, according to Thy prayer, BE IN US. Then shall we say aright, 'Our Father!' Then shall we apprehend Thy teaching, and the first spontaneous breathing of our heart will be: 'Our Father, Thy Name, Thy Kingdom, Thy Will.' And we shall bring our needs and our sins and our temptations to Him in the confidence that the love of such a Father cares for all.

Blessed Lord! we are Thy scholars, we trust Thee; do teach us to pray, 'Our Father.' Amen.

ALL OF GRACE

An Earnest Word with Those

Who Are Seeking Salvation

by the Lord Jesus Christ

By

C.H. SPURGEON

"Where sin abounded,

grace did much more abound."

Romans 5:20

TO YOU

He who spoke and wrote this message will be greatly disappointed if it does not lead many to the Lord Jesus. It is sent forth in childlike dependence upon the power of God the Holy Ghost, to use it in the conversion of millions, if so He pleases. No doubt many poor men and women will take up this little volume, and the Lord will visit them with grace. To answer this end, the very plainest language has been chosen, and many homely expressions have been used. But if those of wealth and rank should glance at this book, the Holy Ghost can impress *them* also; since that which can be understood by the unlettered is none the less attractive to the instructed. Oh that some might read it who will become great winners of souls!

Who knows how many will find their way to peace by what they read here? A more important question to you, dear reader, is this-- *Will you be one of them?*

A certain man placed a fountain by the wayside, and he hung up a cup near to it by a little chain. He was told some time after that a great art-critic had found much fault with its design. "But," said he, "do many thirsty persons drink at it?" Then they told him that thousands of poor people, men, women, and children, slaked their thirst at this fountain; and he smiled and said, that he was little troubled by the critic's observation, only he hoped that on some sultry summer's day the critic himself might fill the cup, and be refreshed, and praise the name of the Lord.

Here is my fountain, and here is my cup: find fault if you please; but *do drink of the water of life*. I only care for this. I had rather bless the soul of the poorest crossing-sweeper, or rag-gatherer, than please a prince of the blood, and fail to convert him to God.

Reader, do you mean business in reading these pages? If so, we are agreed at the outset; but nothing short of your finding Christ and

Heaven is the business aimed at here. Oh that we may seek this together! I do so by dedicating this little book with prayer. Will not you join me by looking up to God, and asking Him to bless you while you read? Providence has put these pages in your way, you have a little spare time in which to read them, and you feel willing to give your attention to them. These are good signs. Who knows but the set time of blessing is come for you? At any rate, "The Holy Ghost saith, Today, if ye will hear his voice, harden not your hearts."

WHAT ARE WE AT?

I heard a story; I think it came from the North Country: A minister called upon a poor woman, intending to give her help; for he knew that she was very poor. With his money in his hand, he knocked at the door; but she did not answer. He concluded she was not at home, and went his way. A little after he met her at the church, and told her that he had remembered her need: "I called at your house, and knocked several times, and I suppose you were not at home, for I had no answer." "At what hour did you call, sir?" "It was about noon." "Oh, dear," she said, "I heard you, sir, and I am so sorry I did not answer; but *I thought it was the man calling for the rent.*" Many a poor woman knows what this meant. Now, it is my desire to be heard, and therefore I want to say that I am not calling for the rent; indeed, it is not the object of this book to ask anything of you, but to tell you that salvation is ALL OF GRACE, which means, *free, gratis, for nothing.*

Oftentimes, when we are anxious to win attention, our hearer thinks, "Ah! now I am going to be told my duty. It is the man calling for that which is due to God, and I am sure I have nothing wherewith to pay. I will not be at home." No, this book does not come to make a demand upon you, but to bring you something. We are not going to talk about law, and duty, and punishment, but about love, and goodness, and forgiveness, and mercy, and eternal life. Do not, therefore, act as if you were not at home: do not turn a deaf ear, or a careless heart. I am asking nothing of you in the name of God or man. It is not my intent to make any requirement at your hands; but I come in God's name, to bring you a free gift, which it shall be to your present and eternal joy to receive. Open the door, and let my pleadings enter. "Come now, and let us reason together." The Lord himself invites you to a conference concerning your immediate and endless happiness, and He would not have done this if He did not mean well toward you. Do not refuse the Lord Jesus who knocks at your door; for He knocks with a hand which was nailed to the tree for such as you are. Since His only and sole object is your good, incline your ear and come to Him. Hearken diligently, and let the good word sink into your soul. It may be that the hour is come in which you shall enter upon that new life which is the beginning of heaven. Faith cometh by hearing, and reading is a sort of hearing: faith may come to you while you are reading this book. Why not? O blessed Spirit of all grace, make it so!

GOD JUSTIFIETH THE UNGODLY

This message is for you. You will find the text in the Epistle to the Romans, in the fourth chapter and the fifth verse:

> *To him that worketh not, but believeth on him that justifieth the ungodly, his faith is counted for righteousness.*

I call your attention to those words, "*Him that justifieth the ungodly.*" They seem to me to be very wonderful words.

Are you not surprised that there should be such an expression as that in the Bible, "That justifieth the ungodly?" I have heard that men that hate the doctrines of the cross bring it as a charge against God, that He saves wicked men and receives to Himself the vilest of the vile. See how this Scripture accepts the charge, and plainly states it! By the mouth of His servant Paul, by the inspiration of the Holy Ghost, He takes to Himself the title of "Him that justifieth the ungodly." He makes those just who are unjust, forgives those who deserve to be punished, and favors those who deserve no favor. You thought, did you not, that salvation was for the good? that God's grace was for the pure and holy, who are free from sin? It has fallen into your mind that, if you were excellent, then God would reward you; and you have thought that because you are not worthy, therefore there could be no way of your enjoying His favor. You must be somewhat surprised to read a text like this: "Him that justifieth the ungodly." I do not wonder that you are surprised; for with all my familiarity with the great grace of God, I never cease to wonder at it. It does sound surprising, does it not, that it should be possible for a holy God to justify an unholy man? We, according to the natural legality of our hearts, are always talking about our own goodness and our own worthiness, and we stubbornly hold to it that there must be somewhat in us in order to win the notice of God. Now, God, who sees through all deceptions, knows that there is no goodness whatever in us. He says that "there is none righteous, no not one." He knows that "all our righteousnesses are as filthy rags," and, therefore the Lord Jesus did not come into the world to look after goodness and righteousness with him, and to bestow them upon persons who have none of them. He comes, not because we *are* just, but to make us so: he justifieth the ungodly.

When a counsellor comes into court, if he is an honest man, he desires to plead the case of an innocent person and justify him before the court from the things which are falsely laid to his charge. It should be the lawyer's object to justify the innocent person, and he should not attempt to screen the guilty party. It lies not in man's right nor in man's power truly to justify the guilty. This is a miracle reserved for the Lord alone. God, the infinitely just Sovereign, knows that there is not a just man upon earth that doeth good and sinneth not, and therefore, in the infinite sovereignty of His divine nature and in the splendor of His ineffable love, He undertakes the task, not so much of justifying the just as of justifying the ungodly. God has devised ways and means of making the ungodly man to stand justly accepted before Him: He has set up a system by which with perfect justice He can treat the guilty as if he had been all his life free from offence, yea, can treat him as if he were wholly free from sin. He justifieth the ungodly.

Jesus Christ came into the world to save *sinners*. It is a very surprising thing--a thing to be marveled at most of all by those who enjoy it. I know that it is to me even to this day the greatest wonder that I ever heard of, that God should ever justify *me*. I feel myself to be a lump of unworthiness, a mass of corruption, and a heap of sin, apart from His almighty love. I know by a full assurance that I am justified by faith which is in Christ Jesus, and treated as if I had been perfectly just, and made an heir of God and a joint heir with Christ; and yet by nature I must take my place among the most sinful. I, who am altogether undeserving, am treated as if I had been deserving. I am loved with as much love as if I had always been godly, whereas aforetime I was ungodly. Who can help being astonished at this? Gratitude for such favor stands dressed in robes of wonder.

Now, while this is very surprising, I want you to notice how available it makes the gospel to you and to me. If God justifieth the *ungodly*, then, dear friend, He can justify *you*. Is not that the very kind of person that you are? If you are unconverted at this moment, it is a very proper description of you; you have lived without God, you have been the reverse of godly; in one word, you have been and are *ungodly*. Perhaps you have not even attended a place of worship on Sunday, but have lived in disregard of God's day, and house, and Word--this proves you to have been ungodly. Sadder still, it may be you have even tried to doubt God's existence, and have gone the length of saying that you did so. You have lived on this fair earth, which is full of the tokens of God's presence, and all the while you have shut your eyes to the clear evidences of His power and Godhead. You have lived as if there were no God. Indeed, you would have been very pleased if you could have demonstrated to yourself to a certainty that there was no God whatever. Possibly you have lived a great many years in this way, so that you are now pretty well settled in your ways, and yet God is not in any of them. If you were labeled

UNGODLY

it would as well describe you as if the sea were to be labeled salt water. Would it not?

Possibly you are a person of another sort; you have regularly attended to all the outward forms of religion, and yet you have had no heart in them at all, but have been really ungodly. Though meeting with the people of God, you have never met with God for yourself; you have been in the choir, and yet have not praised the Lord with your heart. You have lived without any love to God in your heart, or regard to his commands in your life. Well, you are just the kind of man to whom this gospel is sent--this gospel which says that God justifieth *the ungodly*. It is very wonderful, but it is happily available for you. It just suits you. Does it not? How I wish that you would accept it! If you are a sensible man, you will see the remarkable grace of God in providing for such as you are, and you will say to yourself, "Justify the ungodly! Why, then, should not I be justified, and justified at once?"

Now, observe further, that *it must be so*--that the salvation of God is for those who do not deserve it, and have no preparation for it. It is reasonable that the statement should be put in the Bible; for, dear friend, no others need justifying but those who have no justification of their own. If any of my readers are perfectly righteous, they want no justifying. You feel that you are doing your duty well, and almost putting heaven under an obligation to you. What do you want with a

Saviour, or with mercy? What do you want with justification? You will be tired of my book by this time, for it will have no interest to you.

If any of you are giving yourselves such proud airs, listen to me for a little while. You will be lost, as sure as you are alive. You righteous men, whose righteousness is all of your own working, are either deceivers or deceived; for the Scripture cannot lie, and it saith plainly, "There is none righteous, no, not one." In any case I have no gospel to preach to the self-righteous, no, not a word of it. Jesus Christ himself came not to call the righteous, and I am not going to do what He did not do. If I called you, you would not come, and, therefore, I will not call you, under that character. No, I bid you rather look at that righteousness of yours till you see what a delusion it is. It is not half so substantial as a cobweb. Have done with it! Flee from it! Oh believe that the only persons that can need justification are those who are not in themselves just! They need that something should be done for them to make them just before the judgment seat of God. Depend upon it, the Lord only does that which is needful. Infinite wisdom never attempts that which is unnecessary. Jesus never undertakes that which is superfluous. To make him just who *is* just is no work for God--that were a labor for a fool; but to make him just who is unjust--that is work for infinite love and mercy. To justify the ungodly--this is a miracle worthy of a God. And for certain it is so.

Now, look. If there be anywhere in the world a physician who has discovered sure and precious remedies, to whom is that physician sent? To those who are perfectly healthy? I think not. Put him down in a district where there are no sick persons, and he feels that he is not in his place. There is nothing for him to do. "The whole have no need of a physician, but they that are sick." Is it not equally clear that the great remedies of grace and redemption are for the sick in soul? They cannot be for the whole, for they cannot be of use to such. If you, dear friend, feel that you are spiritually sick, the Physician has come into the world for you. If you are altogether undone by reason of your sin, you are the very person aimed at in the plan of salvation. I say that the Lord of love had just such as you are in His eye when He arranged the system of grace. Suppose a man of generous spirit were to resolve to forgive all those who were indebted to him; it is clear that this can only apply to those really in his debt. One person owes him a thousand pounds; another owes him fifty pounds; each one has but to have his bill receipted, and the liability is wiped out. But the most generous person cannot forgive the debts of those who do not owe him anything. It is out of the power of Omnipotence to forgive where there is no sin. Pardon, therefore, cannot be for you who have no sin. Pardon must be for the guilty. Forgiveness must be for the sinful. It were absurd to talk of forgiving those who do not need forgiveness--pardoning those who have never offended.

Do you think that you must be lost because you are a sinner? This is the reason why you can be saved. Because you own yourself to be a sinner I would encourage you to believe that grace is ordained for such as you are. One of our hymn-writers even dared to say:

A sinner is a sacred thing;
The Holy Ghost hath made him so.

It is truly so, that Jesus seeks and saves that which is lost. He died and made a real atonement for real sinners. When men are not playing with words, or calling themselves "miserable sinners," out of mere compliment, I feel overjoyed to meet with them. I would be glad to talk all night to bona fide sinners. The inn of mercy never closes its doors upon such, neither weekdays nor Sunday. Our Lord Jesus did not die for imaginary sins, but His heart's blood was spilt to wash out deep crimson stains, which nothing else can remove.

He that is a black sinner--he is the kind of man that Jesus Christ came to make white. A gospel preacher on one occasion preached a sermon from, "Now also the axe is laid to the root of the trees," and he delivered such a sermon that one of his hearers said to him, "One would have thought that you had been preaching to criminals. Your sermon ought to have been delivered in the county jail." "Oh, no," said the good man, "if I were preaching in the county jail, I should not preach from that text, there I should preach 'This is a faithful saying, and worthy of all acceptation, that Christ Jesus came into the world to save sinners.'" Just so. The law is for the self-righteous, to humble their pride: the gospel is for the lost, to remove their despair.

If you are not lost, what do you want with a Saviour? Should the shepherd go after those who never went astray? Why should the woman sweep her house for the bits of money that were never out of her purse? No, the medicine is for the diseased; the quickening is for the dead; the pardon is for the guilty; liberation is for those who are bound: the opening of eyes is for those who are blind. How can the Saviour, and His death upon the cross, and the gospel of pardon, be accounted for, unless it be upon the supposition that men are guilty and worthy of condemnation? The sinner is the gospel's reason for existence. You, my friend, to whom this word now comes, if you are undeserving, ill-deserving, hell-deserving, you are the sort of man for whom the gospel is ordained, and arranged, and proclaimed. God justifieth the ungodly.

I would like to make this very plain. I hope that I have done so already; but still, plain as it is, it is only the Lord that can make a man see it. It does at first seem most amazing to an awakened man that salvation should really be for him as a lost and guilty one. He thinks that it must be for him as a penitent man, forgetting that his penitence is a part of his salvation. "Oh," says he, "but I must be this and that,"--all of which is true, for he shall be this and that as the result of salvation; but salvation comes to him before he has any of the results of salvation. It comes to him, in fact, while he deserves only this bare, beggarly, base, abominable description, "*ungodly*." That is all he is when God's gospel comes to justify him.

May I, therefore, urge upon any who have no good thing about them--who fear that they have not even a good feeling, or anything whatever that can recommend them to God--that they will firmly believe that our gracious God is able and willing to take them without anything to recommend them, and to forgive them spontaneously, not because *they* are good, but because *He* is good. Does He not make His sun to shine on the evil as well as on the good? Does He not give fruitful seasons, and send the rain and the sunshine in their time upon the most ungodly nations? Ay, even Sodom had its sun, and Gomorrah had its dew. Oh friend, the great grace of God surpasses my conception and your conception, and I would have you think worthily of it! As high as the heavens are above the earth; so high are God's thoughts above our thoughts. He can abundantly pardon. Jesus Christ came into the world to save sinners: forgiveness is for the guilty.

Do not attempt to touch yourself up and make yourself something other than you really are; but come as you are to Him who justifies the ungodly. A great artist some short time ago had painted a part of the corporation of the city in which he lived, and he wanted, for historic purposes, to include in his picture certain characters well known in the town. A crossing-sweeper, unkempt, ragged, filthy, was known to everybody, and there was a suitable place for him in the picture. The artist said to this ragged and rugged individual, "I will pay you well if you will come down to my studio and let me take your likeness." He came round in the morning, but he was soon sent about his business; for he had washed his face, and combed his hair, and donned a respectable suit of clothes. He was needed as a beggar, and was not invited in any other capacity. Even so, the gospel will receive you into its halls if you come as a sinner, not otherwise. Wait not for reformation, but come at once for salvation. God justifieth *the ungodly*, and that takes *you* up where you now are: it meets you in your worst estate.

Come in your *deshabille*. I mean, come to your heavenly Father in all your sin and sinfulness. Come to Jesus just as you are, leprous, filthy, naked, neither fit to live nor fit to die. Come, you that are the very sweepings of creation; come, though you hardly dare to hope for anything but death. Come, though despair is brooding over you, pressing upon your bosom like a horrible nightmare. Come and ask the Lord to justify another ungodly one. Why should He not? Come for this great mercy of God is meant for such as you are. I put it in the language of the text, and I cannot put it more strongly: the Lord God Himself takes to Himself this gracious title, "Him that justifieth the ungodly." He makes just, and causes to be treated as just, those who by nature are ungodly. Is not that a wonderful word *for you*? Reader, do not delay till you have well considered this matter.

"IT IS GOD THAT JUSTIFIETH"

Romans 8:33

A wonderful thing it is, this being justified, or made just. If we had never broken the laws of God we should not have needed it, for we should have been just in ourselves. He who has all his life done the things which he ought to have done, and has never done anything which he ought not to have done, is justified by the law. But you, dear reader, are not of that sort, I am quite sure. You have too much honesty to pretend to be without sin, and therefore you need to be justified.

Now, if you justify yourself, you will simply be a self-deceiver. Therefore do not attempt it. It is never worth while.

If you ask your fellow mortals to justify you, what can they do? You can make some of them speak well of you for small favors, and others will backbite you for less. Their judgment is not worth much.

Our text says, "It is God that justifieth," and this is a deal more to the point. It is an astonishing fact, and one that we ought to consider with care. Come and see.

In the first place, *nobody else but God would ever have thought of justifying those who are guilty*. They have lived in open rebellion; they have done evil with both hands; they have gone from bad to worse; they have turned back to sin even after they have smarted for it, and have therefore for a while been forced to leave it. They have broken the law, and trampled on the gospel. They have refused proclamations of mercy, and have persisted in ungodliness. How can they be forgiven and justified? Their fellowmen, despairing of them, say, "They are hopeless cases." Even Christians look upon them with sorrow rather than with hope. But not so their God. He, in the splendor of his electing grace having chosen some of them before the foundation of the world, will not rest till He has justified them, and made them to be accepted in the Beloved. Is it not written, "Whom he did predestinate, them he also called: and whom he called them he also justified: and whom he justified, them he also glorified"? Thus you see there are some whom the Lord resolves to justify: why should not you and I be of the number?

None but God would ever have thought of justifying *me*. I am a wonder to myself. I doubt not that grace is equally seen in others. Look at Saul of Tarsus, who foamed at the mouth, against God's servants. Like a hungry wolf, he worried the lambs and the sheep right and left; and yet God struck him down on the road to Damascus, and changed his heart, and so fully justified him that ere long, this man became the greatest preacher of justification by faith that ever lived. He must often have marveled that he was justified by faith in Christ Jesus; for he was once a determined stickler for salvation by the works of the law. None but God would have ever thought of justifying such a man as Saul the persecutor; but the Lord God is glorious in grace.

But, even if anybody had thought of justifying the ungodly, *none but God could have done it*. It is quite impossible for any person to forgive offences which have not been committed against himself. A person has greatly injured you; you can forgive him, and I hope you will; but no third person can forgive him apart from you. If the wrong is done to you, the pardon must come from you. If we have sinned against God, it is in God's power to forgive; for the sin is against Himself. That is why David says, in the fifty-first Psalm: "Against thee, thee only, have I sinned, and done this evil in thy sight"; for then God, against whom the offence is committed, can put the offence away. That which we owe to God, our great Creator can remit, if so it pleases Him; and if He remits it, it is remitted. None but the great God, against whom we have committed the sin, can blot out that sin; let us, therefore, see that we go to Him and seek mercy at His hands. Do not let us be led aside by those who would have us confess to them; they have no warrant in the Word of God for their pretensions. But even if they were ordained to pronounce absolution in God's name, it must still be better to go ourselves to the great Lord through Jesus Christ, the Mediator, and seek and find pardon at His hand; since we are sure that this is the right way. Proxy religion involves too great a risk: you had better see to your soul's matters yourself, and leave them in no man's hands.

Only God can justify the ungodly; but *He can do it to perfection*. He casts our sins behind His back, He blots them out; He says that though they be sought for, they shall not be found. With no other reason for it but His own infinite goodness, He has prepared a glorious way by which He can make scarlet sins as white as snow, and remove our transgressions from us as far as the east is from the west. He says, "I will not remember your sins." He goes the length of making an end of sin. One of old called out in amazement, "Who is a God like unto thee, that pardoneth iniquity, and passeth by the transgression of the remnant of his heritage? he retaineth not his anger for ever, because he delighteth in mercy" (Micah 7:18).

We are not now speaking of justice, nor of God's dealing with men according to their deserts. If you profess to deal with the righteous Lord on law terms, everlasting wrath threatens you, for that is what you deserve. Blessed be His name, He has not dealt with us after our sins; but now He treats with us on terms of free grace and infinite compassion, and He says, "I will receive you graciously, and love you freely." Believe it, for it is certainly true that the great God is able to treat the guilty with abundant mercy; yea, He is able to treat the ungodly as if they had been always godly. Read carefully the parable of the prodigal son, and see how the forgiving father received the returning wanderer with as much love as if he had never gone away, and had never defiled himself with harlots. So far did he carry this that the elder brother began to grumble at it; but the father never withdrew his love. Oh my brother, however guilty you may be, if you will only come back to your God and Father, He will treat you as if you had never done wrong! He will regard you as just, and deal with you accordingly. What say you to this?

Do you not see--for I want to bring this out clearly, what a splendid thing it is--that as none but God would think of justifying the ungodly, and none but God could do it, yet the Lord can do it? See how the apostle puts the challenge, "Who shall lay anything to the charge of God's elect? It is God that justifieth." If God has justified a man it is well done, it is rightly done, it is justly done, it is everlastingly done. I read a statement in a magazine which is full of venom against the gospel and those who preach it, that we hold some kind of theory by which we imagine that sin can be removed from men. We hold no theory, we publish a fact. The grandest fact under heaven is this--that Christ by His precious blood does actually put away sin, and that God, for Christ's sake, dealing with men on terms of divine mercy, forgives the guilty and justifies them, not according to anything that He sees in them, or foresees will be in them, but according to the riches of His mercy which lie in His own heart. This we have preached, do preach, and will preach as long as we live. "It is God that justifieth"--that justifieth the ungodly; He is not ashamed of doing it, nor are we of preaching it.

The justification which comes from God himself must be beyond question. If the Judge acquits me, who can condemn me? If the highest court in the universe has pronounced me just, who shall lay anything to my charge? Justification from God is a sufficient answer to an awakened conscience. The Holy Spirit by its means breathes peace over our entire nature, and we are no longer afraid. With this justification we can answer all the roarings and railings of Satan and ungodly men. With this we shall be able to die: with this we shall boldly rise again, and face the last great assize.

> Bold shall I stand in that great day,
> For who aught to my charge shall lay?
> While by my Lord absolved I am
> From sin's tremendous curse and blame.

Friend, *the Lord can blot out all your sins.* I make no shot in the dark when I say this. "All *manner* of sin and of blasphemy shall be forgiven unto men." Though you are steeped up to your throat in crime, He can with a word remove the defilement, and say, "I will, be thou clean." The Lord is a great forgiver.

"I believe in the Forgiveness of Sins." Do You?

He can even at this hour pronounce the sentence, "Thy sins be forgiven thee; go in peace;" and if He do this, no power in Heaven, or earth, or under the earth, can put you under suspicion, much less under wrath. Do not doubt the power of Almighty love. *You* could not forgive your fellow man had he offended you as you have offended God; but you must not measure God's corn with your bushel; His thoughts and ways are as much above yours as the heavens are high above the earth.

"Well," say you, "it would be a great miracle if the Lord were to pardon me." Just so. It would be a supreme miracle, and therefore He is likely to do it; for He does "great things and unsearchable" which we looked not for.

I was myself stricken down with a horrible sense of guilt, which made my life a misery to me; but when I heard the command, "Look unto me, and be ye saved, all the ends of the earth, for I am God and there is none else"--I looked, and in a moment the Lord justified me. Jesus Christ, made sin for me, was what I saw, and that sight gave me rest. When those who were bitten by the fiery serpents in the wilderness looked to the serpent of brass they were healed at once; and so was I when I looked to the crucified Saviour. The Holy Spirit, who enabled me to believe, gave me peace through believing. I felt as sure that I was forgiven, as before I felt sure of condemnation. I had been certain of my condemnation because the Word of God declared it, and my conscience bore witness to it; but when the Lord justified me I was made equally certain by the same witnesses. The word of the Lord in the Scripture saith, "He that believeth on him is not condemned," and my conscience bears witness that I believed, and that God in pardoning me is just. Thus I have the witness of the Holy Spirit and my own conscience, and these two agree in one. Oh, how I wish that my reader would receive the testimony of God upon this matter, and then full soon he would also have the witness in himself!

I venture to say that a sinner justified by God stands on even a surer footing than a righteous man justified by his works, if such there be. We could never be surer that we had done enough works; conscience would always be uneasy lest, after all, we should come short, and we could only have the trembling verdict of a fallible judgment to rely upon; but when God himself justifies, and the Holy Spirit bears witness thereto by giving us peace with God, why then we feel that the matter is sure and settled, and we enter into rest. No tongue can tell the depth of that calm which comes over the soul which has received the peace of God which passeth all understanding.

JUST AND THE JUSTIFIER

We have seen the ungodly justified, and have considered the great truth, that only God can justify any man; we now come a step further and make the inquiry--*How can a just God justify guilty men?* Here we are met with a full answer in the words of Paul, in Romans 3:21-26. We will read six verses from the chapter so as to get the run of the passage:

"But now the righteousness of God without the law is manifested, being witnessed by the law and the prophets; even the righteousness of God which is by faith of Jesus Christ unto all and upon all them that believe: for there is no difference; for all have sinned, and come short of the glory of God; being justified freely by his grace through the redemption that is in Christ Jesus: whom God hath set forth to be a propitiation through faith in his blood, to declare his righteousness for the remission of sins that are past, through the forbearance of God; to declare, I say, at this time his righteousness; that he might be just, and the justifier of him which believeth in Jesus."

Here suffer me to give you a bit of personal experience. When I was under the hand of the Holy Spirit, under conviction of sin, I had a clear and sharp sense of the justice of God. Sin, whatever it might be to other people, became to me an intolerable burden. It was not so much that I feared hell, but that I feared sin. I knew myself to be so horribly guilty that I remember feeling that if God did not punish me for sin He ought to do so. I felt that the Judge of all the earth ought to condemn such sin as mine. I sat on the judgment seat, and I condemned myself to perish; for I confessed that had I been God I could have done no other than send such a guilty creature as I was down to the lowest hell. All the while, I had upon my mind a deep concern for the honor of God's name, and the integrity of His moral government. I felt that it would not satisfy my conscience if I could be forgiven unjustly. The sin I had committed must be punished. But then there was the question how God could be just, and yet justify me who had been so guilty. I asked my heart: "How can He be just and yet the justifier?" I was worried and wearied with this question; neither could I see any answer to it. Certainly, I could never have invented an answer which would have satisfied my conscience.

The doctrine of the atonement is to my mind one of the surest proofs of the divine inspiration of Holy Scripture. Who would or could have thought of the just Ruler dying for the unjust rebel? This is no teaching of human mythology, or dream of poetical imagination. This method of expiation is only known among men because it is a fact; fiction could not have devised it. God Himself ordained it; it is not a matter which could have been imagined.

I had heard the plan of salvation by the sacrifice of Jesus from my youth up; but I did not know any more about it in my innermost soul than if I had been born and bred a Hottentot. The light was there, but I was blind; it was of necessity that the Lord himself should make the matter plain to me. It came to me as a new revelation, as fresh as if I had never read in Scripture that Jesus was declared to be the propitiation for sins that God might be just. I believe it will have to come as a revelation to every newborn child of God whenever he sees it; I mean that glorious doctrine of the substitution of the Lord Jesus. I came to understand that salvation was possible through vicarious sacrifice; and that provision had been made in the first constitution and arrangement of things for such a substitution. I was made to see that He who is the Son of God, co-equal, and co-eternal with the Father, had of old been made the covenant Head of a chosen people that He might in that capacity suffer for them and save them. Inasmuch as our fall was not at the first a personal one, for we fell in our federal representative, the first Adam, it became possible for us to be recovered by a second representative, even by Him who has undertaken to be the covenant head of His people, so as to be their second Adam. I saw that ere I actually sinned I had fallen by my first father's sin; and I rejoiced that therefore it became possible in point of law for me to rise by a second head and representative. The fall by Adam left a loophole of escape; another Adam can undo the ruin made by the first. When I was anxious about the possibility of a just God pardoning me, I understood and saw by faith that He who is the Son of God became man, and in His own blessed person bore my sin in His own body on the tree. I saw the chastisement of my peace was laid on Him, and that with His stripes I was healed. Dear friend, *have you ever seen that?* Have you ever understood how God can be just to the full, not remitting penalty nor blunting the edge of the sword, and yet can be infinitely merciful, and can justify the ungodly who turn to Him? It was because the Son of God, supremely glorious in His matchless person, undertook to vindicate the law by bearing the sentence due to me, that therefore God is able to pass by my sin. The law of God was more vindicated by the death of Christ than it would have been had all transgressors been sent to Hell. For the Son of God to suffer for sin was a more glorious establishment of the government of God, than for the whole race to suffer.

Jesus has borne the death penalty on our behalf. Behold the wonder! There He hangs upon the cross! This is the greatest sight you will ever see. Son of God and Son of Man, there He hangs, bearing pains unutterable, the just for the unjust, to bring us to God. Oh, the glory of that sight! The innocent punished! The Holy One condemned! The Ever-blessed made a curse! The infinitely glorious put to a shameful death! The more I look at the sufferings of the Son of God, the more sure I am that they must meet my case. Why did He suffer, if not to turn aside the penalty from us? If, then, He turned it aside by His death, it is turned aside, and those who believe in Him need not fear it. It must be so, that since expiation is made, God is able to forgive without shaking the basis of His throne, or in the least degree blotting the statute book. Conscience gets a full answer to her tremendous question. The wrath of God against iniquity, whatever that may be, must be beyond all conception terrible. Well did Moses say, "Who knoweth the power of thine anger?" Yet when we hear the Lord of glory cry, "Why hast thou forsaken me?" and see Him yielding up the ghost, we feel that the justice of God has received abundant vindication by obedience so perfect and death so terrible, rendered by so divine a person. If God himself bows before His own law, what more can be done? There is more in the atonement by way of merit, than there is in all human sin by way of demerit.

The great gulf of Jesus' loving self-sacrifice can swallow up the mountains of our sins, all of them. For the sake of the infinite good of this one representative man, the Lord may well look with favor upon other men, however unworthy they may be in and of themselves. It was a miracle of miracles that the Lord Jesus Christ should stand in our stead and

> Bear that we might never bear
> His Father's righteous ire.

But he has done so. "It is finished." God will spare the sinner because He did not spare His Son. God can pass by your transgressions because He laid those transgressions upon His only begotten Son nearly two thousand years ago. If you believe in Jesus (that is the point), then your sins were carried away by Him who was the scapegoat for His people.

What is it to believe in Him? It is not merely to say, "He is God and the Saviour," but to trust Him wholly and entirely, and take Him for all your salvation from this time forth and forever--your Lord, your Master, your all. If you will have Jesus, He has you already. If you believe on Him, I tell you you cannot go to hell; for that were to make the sacrifice of Christ of none effect. It cannot be that a sacrifice should be accepted, and yet the soul should die for whom that sacrifice has been received. If the believing soul could be condemned, then why a sacrifice? If Jesus died in my stead, why should I die also? Every believer can claim that the sacrifice was actually made for him: by faith he has laid his hands on it, and made it his own, and therefore he may rest assured that he can never perish. The Lord would not receive this offering on our behalf, and then condemn us to die. The Lord cannot read our pardon written in the blood of His own Son, and then smite us. That were impossible. Oh that you may have grace given you at once to look away to Jesus and to begin at the beginning, even at Jesus, who is the Fountain-head of mercy to guilty man!

"He justifieth the ungodly." "It is God that justifieth," therefore, and for that reason only it can be done, and He does it through the atoning sacrifice of His divine Son. Therefore it can be justly done--so justly done that none will ever question it--so thoroughly done that in the last tremendous day, when heaven and earth shall pass away, there shall be none that shall deny the validity of the justification. "Who is he that condemneth? It is Christ that died. Who shall lay anything to the charge of God's elect? It is God that justifieth."

Now, poor soul! will you come into this lifeboat, just as you are? Here is safety from the wreck! Accept the sure deliverance. "I have nothing with me," say you. You are not asked to bring anything with you. Men who escape for their lives will leave even their clothes behind. Leap for it, just as you are.

I will tell you this thing about myself to encourage you. My sole hope for heaven lies in the full atonement made upon Calvary's cross for the ungodly. On that I firmly rely. I have not the shadow of a hope anywhere else. You are in the same condition as I am; for we neither of us have anything of our own worth as a ground of trust. Let us join hands and stand together at the foot of the cross, and trust our souls once for all to Him who shed His blood for the guilty. We will be saved by one and the same Saviour. If you perish trusting Him, I must perish too. What can I do more to prove my own confidence in the gospel which I set before you?

CONCERNING DELIVERANCE FROM SINNING

In this place i would say a plain word or two to those who understand the method of justification by faith which is in Christ Jesus, but whose trouble is that they cannot cease from sin. We can never be happy, restful, or spiritually healthy till we become holy. We must be rid of sin; but how is the riddance to be wrought? This is the life-or-death question of many. The old nature is very strong, and they have tried to curb and tame it; but it will not be subdued, and they find themselves, though anxious to be better, if anything growing worse than before. The heart is so hard, the will is so obstinate, the passions are so furious, the thoughts are so volatile, the imagination is so ungovernable, the desires are so wild, that the man feels that he has a den of wild beasts within him, which will eat him up sooner than be ruled by him. We may say of our fallen nature what the Lord said to Job concerning Leviathan: "Wilt thou play with him as with a bird? or wilt thou bind him for thy maidens?" A man might as well hope to hold the north wind in the hollow of his hand as expect to control by his own strength those boisterous powers which dwell within his fallen nature. This is a greater feat than any of the fabled labors of Hercules: God is wanted here.

"*I could believe that Jesus would forgive sin,*" says one, "*but then my trouble is that I sin again, and that I feel such awful tendencies to evil within me.* As surely as a stone, if it be flung up into the air, soon comes down again to the ground, so do I, though I am sent up to heaven by earnest preaching, return again to my insensible state. Alas! I am easily fascinated with the basilisk eyes of sin, and am thus held as under a spell, so that I cannot escape from my own folly."

Dear friend, salvation would be a sadly incomplete affair if it did not deal with this part of our ruined estate. We want to be purified as well as pardoned. Justification without sanctification would not be salvation at all. It would call the leper clean, and leave him to die of his disease; if would forgive the rebellion and allow the rebel to remain an enemy to his king. It would remove the consequences but overlook the cause, and this would leave an endless and hopeless task before us. It would stop the stream for a time, but leave an open fountain of defilement, which would sooner or later break forth with increased power. Remember that the Lord Jesus came to take away sin in three ways; He came to remove *the penalty* of sin, *the power* of sin, and, at last, *the presence* of sin. At once you may reach to the second part--the power of sin may immediately be broken; and so you will be on the road to the third, namely, the removal of the presence of sin. "We know that he was manifested to take away our sins."

The angel said of our Lord, "Thou shalt call his name Jesus, for he shall save his people from their sins." Our Lord Jesus came to destroy in us the works of the devil. That which was said at our Lord's birth was also declared in His death; for when the soldier pierced His side forthwith came there out blood and water, to set forth the double cure by which we are delivered from the guilt and the defilement of sin.

If, however, you are troubled about the power of sin, and about the tendencies of your nature, as you well may be, here is a promise for you. Have faith in it, for it stands in that covenant of grace which is ordered in all things and sure. God, who cannot lie, has said in Ezekiel 36:26:

> *A new heart also will I give you, and a new spirit will I put within you: and I will take away the stony heart out of your flesh, and I will give you an heart of flesh.*

You see, it is all "I will," and "I will." "I will give," and "I will take away." This is the royal style of the King of kings, who is able to accomplish all His will. No word of His shall ever fall to the ground.

The Lord knows right well that you cannot change your own heart, and cannot cleanse your own nature; but He also knows that He can do both. He can cause the Ethiopian to change his skin, and the leopard his spots. Hear this, and be astonished: He can create you a second time; He can cause you to be born again. This is a miracle of grace, but the Holy Ghost will perform it. It would be a very wonderful thing if one could stand at the foot of the Niagara Falls, and could speak a word which should make the river Niagara begin to run up stream, and leap up that great precipice over which it now rolls in stupendous force. Nothing but the power of God could achieve that marvel; but that would be more than a fit parallel to what would take place if the course of your nature were altogether reversed. All things are possible with God. He can reverse the direction of your desires and the current of your life, and instead of going downward from God, He can make your whole being tend upward toward God. That is, in fact, what the Lord has promised to do for all who are in the covenant; and we know from Scripture that all believers are in the covenant. Let me read the words again:

> *A new spirit will I put within you: and I will take away the stony heart out of your flesh, and will give an heart of flesh. (Ezekiel 11:19).*

What a wonderful promise! And it is yea and amen in Christ Jesus to the glory of God by us. Let us lay hold of it; accept it as true, and appropriate it to ourselves. Then shall it be fulfilled in us, and we shall have, in after days and years, to sing of that wondrous change which the sovereign grace of God has wrought in us.

It is well worthy of consideration that when the Lord takes away the stony heart, that deed is done; and when that is once done, no known power can ever take away that new heart which He gives, and that right spirit which He puts within us. "The gifts and calling of God are without repentance"; that is, without repentance on His part; He does not take away what He once has given. Let Him renew you and you will be renewed. Man's reformations and cleanings up soon come to an end, for the dog returns to his vomit; but when God puts a new heart into us, the new heart is there forever, and never will it harden into stone again. He who made it flesh will keep it so. Herein we may rejoice and be glad forever in that which God creates in the kingdom of His grace.

To put the matter very simply--did you ever hear of Mr. Rowland Hill's illustration of the cat and the sow? I will give it in my own fashion, to illustrate our Saviour's expressive words--"Ye must be born again." Do you see that cat? What a cleanly creature she is! How cleverly she washes herself with her tongue and her paws! It is quite a pretty sight! Did you ever see a sow do that? No, you never did. It is contrary to its nature. It prefers to wallow in the mire. Go and teach a sow to wash itself, and see how little success you would gain. It would be a great sanitary improvement if swine would be clean. Teach them to wash and clean themselves as the cat has been doing! Useless task. You may by force wash that sow, but it hastens to the mire, and is soon as foul as ever. The only way in which you can get a sow to wash itself is to transform it into a cat; then it will wash and be clean, but not till then! Suppose that transformation to be accomplished, and then what was difficult or impossible is easy enough; the swine will henceforth be fit for your parlor and your hearth-rug. So it is with an ungodly man; you cannot force him to do what a renewed man does most willingly; you may teach him, and set him a good example, but he cannot learn the art of holiness, for he has no mind to it; his nature leads him another way. When the Lord makes a new man of him, then all things wear a different aspect. So great is this change, that I once heard a convert say, "Either all the world is changed, or else I am." The new nature follows after right as naturally as the old nature wanders after wrong. What a blessing to receive such a nature! Only the Holy Ghost can give it.

Did it ever strike you what a wonderful thing it is for the Lord to give a new heart and a right spirit to a man? You have seen a lobster, perhaps, which has fought with another lobster, and lost one of its claws, and a new claw has grown. That is a remarkable thing; but it is a much more astounding fact that a man should have a new heart given to him. This, indeed, is a miracle beyond the powers of nature. There is a tree. If you cut off one of its limbs, another one may grow in its place; but can you change the tree; can you sweeten sour sap; can you make the thorn bear figs? You can graft something better into it and that is the analogy which nature gives us of the work of grace; but absolutely to change the vital sap of the tree would be a miracle indeed. Such a prodigy and mystery of power God works in all who believe in Jesus.

If you yield yourself up to His divine working, the Lord will alter your nature; He will subdue the old nature, and breathe new life into you. Put your trust in the Lord Jesus Christ, and He will take the stony heart out of your flesh, and He will give you a heart of flesh. Where everything was hard, everything shall be tender; where everything was vicious, everything shall be virtuous: where everything tended downward, everything shall rise upward with impetuous force. The lion of anger shall give place to the lamb of meekness; the raven of uncleanness shall fly before the dove of purity; the vile serpent of deceit shall be trodden under the heel of truth.

I have seen with my own eyes such marvellous changes of moral and spiritual character that I despair of none. I could, if it were fitting, point out those who were once unchaste women who are now pure as the driven snow, and blaspheming men who now delight all around them by their intense devotion. Thieves are made honest, drunkards sober, liars truthful, and scoffers zealous. Wherever the grace of God has appeared to a man it has trained him to deny ungodliness and worldly lusts, and to live soberly, righteously, and godly in this present evil world: and, dear reader, *it will do the same for you.*

"*I cannot make this change*," says one. Who said you could? The Scripture which we have quoted speaks not of what *man* will do, but of what *God* will do. It is God's promise, and it is for Him to fulfill His own engagements. Trust in Him to fulfill His Word to you, and it will be done.

"But how is it to be done?" What business is that of yours? Must the Lord explain His methods before you will believe him? The Lord's working in this matter is a great mystery: the Holy Ghost performs it. He who made the promise has the responsibility of keeping the promise, and He is equal to the occasion. God, who promises this marvellous change, will assuredly carry it out in all who receive Jesus, for to all such He gives power to become the Sons of God. Oh that you would believe it! Oh that you would do the gracious Lord the justice to believe that He can and will do this for you, great miracle though it will be! Oh that you would believe that God cannot lie! Oh that you would trust Him for a new heart, and a right spirit, for He can give them to you! May the Lord give you faith in His promise, faith in His Son, faith in the Holy Spirit, and faith in Him, and to Him shall be praise and honor and glory forever and ever! Amen.

BY GRACE THROUGH FAITH

"By grace are ye saved, through faith" (Ephesians 2:8).

I think it well to turn a little to one side that I may ask my reader to observe adoringly *the fountain-head* of our salvation, which is the grace of God. "By grace are ye saved." Because God is gracious, therefore sinful men are forgiven, converted, purified, and saved. It is not because of anything in them, or that ever can be in them, that they are saved; but because of the boundless love, goodness, pity, compassion, mercy, and grace of God. Tarry a moment, then, at the well-head. Behold the pure river of water of life, as it proceeds out of the throne of God and of the Lamb!

What an abyss is the grace of God! Who can measure its breadth? Who can fathom its depth? Like all the rest of the divine attributes, it is infinite. God is full of love, for "God is love." God is full of goodness; the very name "God" is short for "good." Unbounded goodness and love enter into the very essence of the Godhead. It is because "his mercy endureth for ever" that men are not destroyed; because "his compassions fail not" that sinners are brought to Him and forgiven.

Remember this; or you may fall into error by fixing your minds so much upon the faith which is the channel of salvation as to forget the grace which is the fountain and source even of faith itself. Faith is the work of God's grace in us. No man can say that Jesus is the Christ but by the Holy Ghost. "No man cometh unto me," saith Jesus, "except the Father which hath sent me draw him." So that faith, which is coming to Christ, is the result of divine drawing. Grace is the first and last moving cause of salvation; and faith, essential as it is, is only an important part of the machinery which grace employs. We are saved "through faith," but salvation is "by grace." Sound forth those words as with the archangel's trumpet: "By grace are ye saved." What glad tidings for the undeserving!

Faith occupies the position of *a channel* or *conduit pipe*. Grace is the fountain and the stream; faith is the aqueduct along which the flood of mercy flows down to refresh the thirsty sons of men. It is a great pity when the aqueduct is broken. It is a sad sight to see around Rome the many noble aqueducts which no longer convey water into the city, because the arches are broken and the marvelous structures are in ruins. The aqueduct must be kept entire to convey the current; and, even so, faith must be true and sound, leading right up to God and coming right down to ourselves, that it may become a serviceable channel of mercy to our souls.

Still, I again remind you that faith is only the channel or aqueduct, and not the fountainhead, and we must not look so much to it as to exalt it above the divine source of all blessing which lies in the grace of God. *Never make a Christ out of your faith*, nor think of as if it were the independent source of your salvation. Our life is found in "looking unto Jesus," not in looking to our own faith. By faith all things become possible to us; yet the power is not in the faith, but in the God upon whom faith relies. Grace is the powerful engine, and faith is the chain by which the carriage of the soul is attached to the great motive power. The righteousness of faith is not the moral excellence of faith, but the righteousness of Jesus Christ which faith grasps and appropriates. The peace within the soul is not derived from the contemplation of our own faith; but it comes to us from Him who is our peace, the hem of whose garment faith touches, and virtue comes out of Him into the soul.

See then, dear friend, that the weakness of your faith will not destroy you. A trembling hand may receive a golden gift. The Lord's salvation can come to us though we have only faith as a grain of mustard seed. The power lies in the grace of God, and not in our faith. Great messages can be sent along slender wires, and the peace-giving witness of the Holy Spirit can reach the heart by means of a thread-like faith which seems almost unable to sustain its own weight. Think more of Him to whom you look than of the look itself. You must look away even from your own looking, and see nothing but Jesus, and the grace of God revealed in Him.

FAITH, WHAT IS IT?

What is this faith concerning which it is said, "By grace are ye saved, *through faith?*" There are many descriptions of faith; but almost all the definitions I have met with have made me understand it less than I did before I saw them. The Negro said, when he read the chapter, that he would *confound* it; and it is very likely that he did so, though he meant to *expound* it. We may explain faith till nobody understands it. I hope I shall not be guilty of that fault. Faith is the simplest of all things, and perhaps because of its simplicity it is the more difficult to explain.

What is faith? *It is made up of three things--knowledge, belief, and trust. Knowledge* comes first. "How shall they believe in him of whom they have not heard?" I want to be informed of a fact before I can possibly believe it. "Faith cometh by hearing"; we must first hear, in order that we may know what is to be believed. "They that know thy name shall put their trust in thee." A measure of knowledge is essential to faith; hence the importance of getting knowledge. "Incline your ear, and come unto me; hear, and your soul shall live." Such was the word of the ancient prophet, and it is the word of the gospel still. Search the Scriptures and learn what the Holy Spirit teacheth concerning Christ and His salvation. Seek to know God: "For he that cometh to God must believe that he is, and that he is a rewarder of them that diligently seek him." May the Holy Spirit give you the spirit of knowledge, and of the fear of the Lord! Know the gospel: know what the good news is, how it talks of free forgiveness, and of change of heart, of adoption into the family of God, and of countless other blessings. Know especially Christ Jesus the Son of God, the Saviour of men, united to us by His human nature, and yet one with God; and thus able to act as Mediator between God and man, able to lay His hand upon both, and to be the connecting link between the sinner and the Judge of all the earth. Endeavour to know more and more of Christ Jesus. Endeavour especially to know the doctrine of the sacrifice of Christ; for the point upon which saving faith mainly fixes itself is this--"God was in Christ, reconciling the world unto himself, not imputing their trespasses unto them." Know that Jesus was "made a curse for us, as it is written, Cursed is every one that hangeth on a tree." Drink deep of the doctrine of the substitutionary work of Christ; for therein lies the sweetest possible comfort to the guilty sons of men, since the Lord "made him to be sin for us, that we might be made the righteousness of God in him." Faith begins with knowledge.

The mind goes on to *believe* that these things are true. The soul believes that God is, and that He hears the cries of sincere hearts; that the gospel is from God; that justification by faith is the grand truth which God hath revealed in these last days by His Spirit more clearly than before. Then the heart believes that Jesus is verily and in truth our God and Saviour, the Redeemer of men, the Prophet, Priest, and King of His people. All this is accepted as sure truth, not to be called in question. I pray that you may at once come to this. Get firmly to believe that "the blood of Jesus Christ, God's dear Son, cleanseth us from all sin"; that His sacrifice is complete and fully accepted of God on man's behalf, so that he that believeth on Jesus is not condemned. Believe these truths as you believe any other statements; for the difference between common faith and saving faith lies mainly in the subjects upon which it is exercised. Believe the witness of God just as you believe the testimony of your own father or friend. "If we receive the witness of men, the witness of God is greater."

So far you have made an advance toward faith; only one more ingredient is needed to complete it, which is *trust*. Commit yourself to the merciful God; rest your hope on the gracious gospel; trust your soul on the dying and living Saviour; wash away your sins in the atoning blood; accept His perfect righteousness, and all is well. Trust is the lifeblood of faith; there is no saving faith without it. The Puritans were accustomed to explain faith by the word "recumbency." It meant leaning upon a thing. Lean with all your weight upon Christ. It would be a better illustration still if I said, fall at full length, and lie on the Rock of Ages. Cast yourself upon Jesus; rest in Him; commit yourself to Him. That done, you have exercised saving faith. Faith is not a blind thing; for faith begins with knowledge. It is not a speculative thing; for faith believes facts of which it is sure. It is not an unpractical, dreamy thing;

for faith trusts, and stakes its destiny upon the truth of revelation. That is one way of describing what faith is.

Let me try again. *Faith is believing that Christ is what He is said to be, and that He will do what He has promised to do, and then to expect this of Him.* The Scriptures speak of Jesus Christ as being God, God is human flesh; as being perfect in His character; as being made of a sin-offering on our behalf; as bearing our sins in His own body on the tree. The Scripture speaks of Him as having finished transgression, made an end of sin, and brought in everlasting righteousness. The sacred records further tell us that He "rose again from the dead," that He "ever liveth to make intercession for us," that He has gone up into the glory, and has taken possession of Heaven on the behalf of His people, and that He will shortly come again "to judge the world in righteousness, and his people with equity." We are most firmly to believe that it is even so; for this is the testimony of God the Father when He said, "This is my beloved Son; hear ye him." This also is testified by God the Holy Spirit; for the Spirit has borne witness to Christ, both in the inspired Word and by divers miracles, and by His working in the hearts of men. We are to believe this testimony to be true.

Faith also believes that Christ will do what He has promised; that since He has promised to cast out none that come to Him, it is certain that He will not cast *us* out if we come to Him. Faith believes that since Jesus said, "The water that I shall give him shall be in him a well of water springing up into everasting life, it must be true; and if *we* get this living Water from Christ it will abide in *us*, and will well up within *us* in streams of holy life. Whatever Christ has promised to do He will do, and we must believe this, so as to look for pardon, justification, preservation, and eternal glory from His hands, according as He has promised them to believers in Him.

Then comes the next necessary step. Jesus is what He is said to be, Jesus will do what He says He will do; therefore we must each one *trust Him*, saying, "He will be to me what He says He is, and He will do to me what He has promised to do; I leave myself in the hands of Him who is appointed to save, that He may save me. I rest upon His promise that He will do even as He has said." This is a saving faith, and he that hath it hath everlasting life. Whatever his dangers and difficulties, whatever his darkness and depression, whatever his infirmities and sins, he that believeth thus on Christ Jesus is not condemned, and shall never come into condemnation.

May that explanation be of some service! I trust it may be used by the Spirit of God to direct my reader into immediate peace. "Be not afraid; only believe." Trust, and be at rest.

My fear is lest the reader should rest content with understanding what is to be done, and yet never do it. Better the poorest real faith actually at work, than the best ideal of it left in the region of speculation. The great matter is to believe on the Lord Jesus *at once*. Never mind distinctions and definitions. A hungry man eats though he does not understand the composition of his food, the anatomy of his mouth, or the process of digestion: he lives because he eats. Another far more clever person understands thoroughly the science of nutrition; but if he does not eat he will die, with all his knowledge. There are, no doubt, many at this hour in Hell who understood the doctrine of faith, but did not believe. On the other hand, not one who has trusted in the Lord Jesus has ever been cast out, though he may never have been able intelligently to define his faith. Oh dear reader, receive the Lord Jesus into your soul, and you shall live forever! "He that believeth in Him hath everlasting life."

HOW MAY FAITH BE ILLUSTRATED?

To make the matter of faith clearer still, I will give you a few illustrations. Though the Holy Spirit alone can make my reader see, it is my duty and my joy to furnish all the light I can, and to pray the divine Lord to open blind eyes. Oh that my reader would pray the same prayer for himself!

The faith which saves has its analogies in the human frame.

It is *the eye* which looks. By the eye we bring into the mind that which is far away; we can bring the sun and the far-off stars into the mind by a glance of the eye. So by trust we bring the Lord Jesus near to us; and though He be far away in Heaven, He enters into our heart. Only look to Jesus; for the hymn is strictly true--

There is life in a look at the Crucified One,

There is life at this moment for thee.

Faith is *the hand* which grasps. When our hand takes hold of anything for itself, it does precisely what faith does when it appropriates Christ and the blessings of His redemption. Faith says, "Jesus is mine." Faith hears of the pardoning blood, and cries, "I accept it to pardon *me*." Faith calls the legacies of the dying Jesus her own; and they are her own, for faith is Christ's heir; He has given Himself and all that He has to faith. Take, O friend, that which grace has provided for thee. You will not be a thief, for you have a divine permit: "Whosoever will, let him take the water of life freely." He who may have a treasure simply by his grasping it will be foolish indeed if he remains poor.

Faith is the *mouth* which feeds upon Christ. Before food can nourish us, it must be received into us. This is a simple matter--this eating and drinking. We willingly receive into the mouth that which is our food, and then we consent that it should pass down into our inward parts, wherein it is taken up and absorbed into our bodily frame. Paul says, in his Epistle to the Romans, in the tenth chapter, "The word is nigh thee, even in thy mouth." Now then, all that is to be done is to swallow it, to suffer it to go down into the soul. Oh that men had an appetite! For he who is hungry and sees meat before him does not need to be taught how to eat. "Give me," said one, "a knife and a fork and a chance." He was fully prepared to do the rest. Truly, a heart which hungers and thirsts after Christ has but to know that He is freely given, and at once it will receive Him. If my reader is in such a case, let him not hesitate to receive Jesus; for he may be sure that he will never be blamed for doing so: for unto "as many as received him, to them gave he power to become the sons of God." He never repulses one, but He authorizes all who come to remain sons for ever.

The pursuits of life illustrate faith in many ways. The farmer buries good seed in the earth, and expects it not only to live but to be multiplied. He has faith in the covenant arrangement, that "seed-time and harvest shall not cease," and he is rewarded for his faith.

The merchant places his money in the care of a banker, and trusts altogether to the honesty and soundness of the bank. He entrusts his capital to another's hands, and feels far more at ease than if he had the solid gold locked up in an iron safe.

The sailor trusts himself to the sea. When he swims he takes his foot from the bottom and rests upon the buoyant ocean. He could not swim if he did not wholly cast himself upon the water.

The goldsmith puts precious metal into the fire which seems eager to consume it, but he receives it back again from the furnace purified by the heat.

You cannot turn anywhere in life without seeing faith in operation between man and man, or between man and natural law. Now, just as we trust in daily life, even so are we to trust in God as He is revealed in Christ Jesus.

Faith exists in different persons in various degrees, according to the amount of their knowledge or growth in grace. Sometimes faith is little more than a simple *clinging* to Christ; a sense of dependence and a willingness so to depend. When you are down at the seaside you will see limpets sticking to the rock. You walk with a soft tread up to the rock; you strike the mollusk a rapid blow with your walking-stick and off he comes. Try the next limpet in that way. You have given him warning; he heard the blow with which you struck his neighbor, and he clings with all his might. You will never get him off; not you! Strike, and strike again, but you may as soon break the rock. Our little friend, the limpet, does not know much, but he clings. He is not acquainted with the geological formation of the rock, but he clings. He can cling, and he has found something to cling to: this is all his stock of knowledge, and he uses it for his security and salvation. It is the limpet's life to cling to the rock, and it is the sinner's life to cling to Jesus. Thousands of God's people have no more faith than this; they know enough to cling to Jesus with all their heart and soul, and this suffices for present peace and eternal safety. Jesus Christ is to them a Saviour strong and mighty, a Rock immovable and immutable; they cling to him for dear life, and this clinging saves them. Reader, cannot you cling? Do so at once.

Faith is seen when one man relies upon another from a knowledge of the superiority of the other. This is a higher faith; the faith which knows the reason for its dependence, and acts upon it. I do not think the limpet knows much about the rock: but as faith grows it becomes more and more intelligent. A blind man trusts himself with his guide because he knows that his friend can see, and, trusting, he walks where his guide conducts him. If the poor man is born blind he does not know what sight is; but he knows that there is such a thing as sight, and that it is possessed by his friend and therefore he freely puts his hand into the hand of the seeing one, and follows his leadership. "We walk by faith, not by sight." "Blessed are they which have not seen, and yet have believed." This is as good an image of faith as well can be; we know that Jesus has about Him merit, and power, and blessing, which we do not possess, and therefore we gladly trust ourselves to Him to be to us what we cannot be to ourselves. We trust Him as the blind man trusts his guide. He never betrays our confidence; but He "is made of God unto us wisdom, and righteousness, and sanctification, and redemption."

Every boy that goes to school has to exert faith while learning. His schoolmaster teaches him geography, and instructs him as to the form of the earth, and the existence of certain great cities and empires. The boy does not himself know that these things are true, except that he believes his teacher, and the books put into his hands. That is what you will have to do with Christ, if you are to be saved; you must simply know because He tells you, believe because He assures you it is even so, and trust yourself with Him because He promises you that salvation will be the result. Almost all that you and I know has come to us by faith. A scientific discovery has been made, and we are sure of it. On what grounds do we believe it? On the authority of certain well-known men of learning, whose reputations are established. We have never made or seen their experiments, but we believe their witness. You must do the like with regard to Jesus: because He teaches you certain truths you are to be His disciple, and believe His words; because He has performed certain acts you are to be His client, and trust yourself with Him. He is infinitely superior to you, and presents himself to your confidence as your Master and Lord. If you will receive Him and His words you shall be saved.

Another and a higher form of faith is that faith which *grows out of love*. Why does a boy trust his father? The reason why the child trusts his father is because he loves him. Blessed and happy are they who have a sweet faith in Jesus, intertwined with deep affection for Him, for this is a restful confidence. These lovers of Jesus are charmed with His character, and delighted with His mission, they are carried away by the lovingkindness that He has manifested, and therefore they cannot help trusting Him, because they so much admire, revere, and love Him.

The way of loving trust in the Saviour may thus be illustrated. A lady is the wife of the most eminent physician of the day. She is seized with a dangerous illness, and is smitten down by its power; yet she is wonderfully calm and quiet, for her husband has made this disease his special study, and has healed thousands who were similarly afflicted. She is not in the least troubled, for she feels perfectly safe in the hands of one so dear to her, and in whom skill and love are blended in their highest forms. Her faith is reasonable and natural; her husband, from every point of view, deserves it of her. This is the kind of faith which the happiest of believers exercise toward Christ. There is no physician like Him, none can save as He can; we love Him, and He loves us, and therefore we put ourselves into His hands, accept whatever He prescribes, and do whatever He bids. We feel that nothing can be wrongly ordered while He is the director of our affairs; for He loves us too well to let us perish, or suffer a single needless pang.

Faith is the root of obedience, and this may be clearly seen in the affairs of life. When a captain trusts a pilot to steer his vessel into port he manages the vessel according to his direction. When a traveler trusts a guide to conduct him over a difficult pass, he follows the track which his guide points out. When a patient believes in a physician, he carefully follows his prescriptions and directions. Faith which refuses to obey the commands of the Saviour is a mere pretence, and will never save the soul. We trust Jesus to save us; He gives us directions as to the way of salvation; we follow those directions and are saved. Let not my reader forget this. Trust Jesus, and prove your trust by doing whatever He bids you.

A notable form of faith *arises out of assured knowledge*; this comes of growth in grace, and is the faith which believes Christ because it knows Him, and trusts Him because it has proved Him to be infallibly faithful. An old Christian was in the habit of writing T and P in the margin of her Bible whenever she had tried and proved a promise. How easy it is to trust a tried and proved Saviour! You cannot do this as yet, but you will do so. Everything must have a beginning. You will rise to strong faith in due time. This matured faith asks not for signs and tokens, but bravely believes. Look at the faith of the master mariner--I have often wondered at it. He looses his cable, he steams away from the land. For days, weeks, or even months, he never sees sail or shore; yet on he goes day and night without fear, till one morning he finds himself exactly opposite to the desired haven toward which he has been steering. How has he found his way over the trackless deep? He has trusted in his compass, his nautical almanac, his glass, and the heavenly bodies; and obeying their guidance, without sighting land, he has steered so accurately that he has not to change a point to enter into port. It is a wonderful thing--that sailing or steaming without sight. Spiritually it is a blessed thing to leave altogether the shores of sight and feeling, and to say, "Good-by" to inward feelings, cheering providences, signs, tokens, and so forth. It is glorious to be far out on the ocean of divine love, believing in God, and steering for Heaven straight away by the direction of the Word of God. "Blessed are they that have not seen, and yet have believed"; to them shall be administered an abundant entrance at the last, and a safe voyage on the way. Will not my reader put his trust in God in Christ Jesus. There I rest with joyous confidence. Brother, come with me, and believe our Father and our Saviour. Come at once.

WHY ARE WE SAVED BY FAITH?

Why is faith selected as the channel of salvation? No doubt this inquiry is often made. "By grace are ye saved *through faith*," is assuredly the doctrine of Holy Scripture, and the ordinance of God; but why is it so? Why is faith selected rather than hope, or love, or patience?

It becomes us to be modest in answering such a question, for God's ways are not always to be understood; nor are we allowed presumptuously to question them. Humbly we would reply that, as far as we can tell, faith has been selected as the channel of grace, because *there is a natural adaptation* in faith to be used as the receiver. Suppose that I am about to give a poor man an alms: I put it into his hand--why? Well, it would hardly be fitting to put it into his ear, or to lay it upon his foot; the hand seems made on purpose to receive. So, in our mental frame, faith is created on purpose to be a receiver: it is the hand of the man, and there is a fitness in receiving grace by its means.

Do let me put this very plainly. Faith which receives Christ is as simple an act as when your child receives an apple from you, because you hold it out and promise to give him the apple if he comes for it. The belief and the receiving relate only to an apple; but they make up precisely the same act as the faith which deals with eternal salvation. What the child's hand is to the apple, that your faith is to the perfect salvation of Christ. The child's hand does not make the apple, nor improve the apple, nor deserve the apple; it only takes it; and faith is chosen by God to be the receiver of salvation, because it does not pretend to create salvation, nor to help in it, but it is content humbly to receive it. "Faith is the tongue that begs pardon, the hand which receives it, and the eye which sees it; but it is not the price which buys it." Faith never makes herself her own plea, she rests all her argument upon the blood of Christ. She becomes a good servant to bring the riches of the Lord Jesus to the soul, because she acknowledges whence she drew them, and owns that grace alone entrusted her with them.

Faith, again, is doubtless selected because *it gives all the glory to God*. It is of faith that it might be by grace, and it is of grace that there might be no boasting; for God cannot endure pride. "The proud he knoweth afar off," and He has no wish to come nearer to them. He will not give salvation in a way which will suggest or foster pride. Paul saith, "Not of works, lest any man should boast." Now, faith excludes all boasting. The hand which receives charity does not say, "I am to be thanked for accepting the gift"; that would be absurd. When the hand conveys bread to the mouth it does not say to the body, "Thank me; for I feed you." It is a very simple thing that the hand does though a very necessary thing; and it never arrogates glory to itself for what it does. So God has selected faith to receive the unspeakable gift of His grace, because it cannot take to itself any credit, but must adore the gracious God who is the giver of all good. Faith sets the crown upon the right head, and therefore the Lord Jesus was wont to put the crown upon the head of faith, saying, "Thy faith hath saved thee; go in peace."

Next, God selects faith as the channel of salvation because *it is a sure method, linking man with God*. When man confides in God, there is a point of union between them, and that union guarantees blessing. Faith saves us because it makes us cling to God, and so brings us into connection with Him. I have often used the following illustration, but I must repeat it, because I cannot think of a better. I am told that years ago a boat was upset above the falls of Niagara, and two men were being carried down the current, when persons on the shore managed to float a rope out to them, which rope was seized by them both. One of them held fast to it and was safely drawn to the bank; but the other, seeing a great log come floating by, unwisely let go the rope and clung to the log, for it was the bigger thing of the two, and apparently better to cling to. Alas! the log with the man on it went right over the vast abyss, because there was no union between the log and the shore. The size of the log was no benefit to him who grasped it; it needed a connection with the shore to produce safety. So when a man trusts to his works, or to sacraments, or to anything of that sort, he will not be saved, because there is no junction between him and Christ; but faith, though it may seem to be like a slender cord, is in the hands of the great God on the shore side; infinite power pulls in the connecting line, and thus draws the man from destruction. Oh the blessedness of faith, because it unites us to God!

Faith is chosen again, because *it touches the springs of action.* Even in common things faith of a certain sort lies at the root of all. I wonder whether I shall be wrong if I say that we never do anything except through faith of some sort. If I walk across my study it is because I believe my legs will carry me. A man eats because he believes in the necessity of food; he goes to business because he believes in the value of money; he accepts a check because he believes that the bank will honor it. Columbus discovered America because he believed that there was another continent beyond the ocean; and the Pilgrim Fathers colonized it because they believed that God would be with them on those rocky shores. Most grand deeds have been born of faith; for good or for evil, faith works wonders by the man in whom it dwells. Faith in its natural form is an all-prevailing force, which enters into all manner of human actions. Possibly he who derides faith in God is the man who in an evil form has the most of faith; indeed, he usually falls into a credulity which would be ridiculous, if it were not disgraceful. God gives salvation to faith, because by creating faith in us He thus touches the real mainspring of our emotions and actions. He has, so to speak, taken possession of the battery and now He can send the sacred current to every part of our nature. When we believe in Christ, and the heart has come into the possession of God, then we are saved from sin, and are moved toward repentance, holiness, zeal, prayer, consecration, and every other gracious thing. "What oil is to the wheels, what weights are to a clock, what wings are to a bird, what sails are to a ship, that faith is to all holy duties and services." Have faith, and all other graces will follow and continue to hold their course.

Faith, again, *has the power of working by love*; it influences the affections toward God, and draws the heart after the best things. He that believes in God will beyond all question love God. Faith is an act of the understanding; but it also proceeds from the heart. "With the heart man believeth unto righteousness"; and hence God gives salvation to faith because it resides next door to the affections, and is near akin to love; and love is the parent and the nurse of every holy feeling and act. Love to God is obedience, love to God is holiness. To love God and to love man is to be conformed to the image of Christ; and this is salvation.

Moreover, *faith creates peace and joy*; he that hath it rests, and is tranquil, is glad and joyous, and this is a preparation for heaven. God gives all heavenly gifts to faith, for this reason among others, that faith worketh in us the life and spirit which are to be eternally manifested in the upper and better world. Faith furnishes us with armor for this life, and education for the life to come. It enables a man both to live and to die without fear; it prepares both for action and for suffering; and hence the Lord selects it as a most convenient medium for conveying grace to us, and thereby securing us for glory.

Certainly faith does for us what nothing else can do; it gives us joy and peace, and causes us to enter into rest. Why do men attempt to gain salvation by other means? An old preacher says, "A silly servant who is bidden to open a door, sets his shoulder to it and pushes with all his might; but the door stirs not, and he cannot enter, use what strength he may. Another comes with a key, and easily unlocks the door, and enters right readily. Those who would be saved by works are pushing at heaven's gate without result; but faith is the key which opens the gate at once." Reader, will you not use that key? The Lord commands you to believe in His dear Son, therefore you may do so; and doing so you shall live. Is not this the promise of the gospel, "He that believeth and is baptized shall be saved"? (Mark 16:16). What can be your objection to a way of salvation which commends itself to the mercy and the wisdom of our gracious God?

ALAS! I CAN DO NOTHING!

After the anxious heart has accepted the doctrine of atonement, and learned the great truth that salvation is by faith in the Lord Jesus, it is often sore troubled with a sense of inability toward that which is good. Many are groaning, "I can do nothing." They are not making this into an excuse, but they feel it as a daily burden. They would if they could. They can each one honestly say, "To will is present with me, but how to perform that which I would I find not."

This feeling seems to make all the gospel null and void; for what is the use of food to a hungry man if he cannot get at it? Of what avail is the river of the water of life if one cannot drink? We recall the story of the doctor and the poor woman's child. The sage practitioner told the mother that her little one would soon be better under proper treatment, but it was absolutely needful that her boy should regularly drink the best wine, and that he should spend a season at one of the German spas. This, to a widow who could hardly get bread to eat! Now, it sometimes seems to the troubled heart that the simple gospel of "Believe and live," is not, after all, so very simple; for it asks the poor sinner to do what he cannot do. To the really awakened, but half instructed, there appears to be a missing link; yonder is the salvation of Jesus, but how is it to be reached? The soul is without strength, and knows not what to do. It lies within sight of the city of refuge, and cannot enter its gate.

Is this want of strength provided for in the plan of salvation? It is. The work of the Lord is perfect. It begins where we are, and asks nothing of us in order to its completion. When the good Samaritan saw the traveler lying wounded and half dead, he did not bid him rise and come to him, and mount the ass and ride off to the inn. No, "he came where he was," and ministered to him, and lifted him upon the beast and bore him to the inn. Thus doth the Lord Jesus deal with us in our low and wretched estate.

We have seen that God justifieth, that He justifieth the ungodly and that He justifies them through faith in the precious blood of Jesus; we have now to see the condition these ungodly ones are in when Jesus works out their salvation. Many awakened persons are not only troubled about their sin, but about their moral weakness. They have no strength with which to escape from the mire into which they have fallen, nor to keep out of it in after days. They not only lament over what they have done, but over what they cannot do. They feel themselves to be powerless, helpless, and spiritually lifeless. It may sound odd to say that they feel dead, and yet it is even so. They are, in their own esteem, to all good incapable. They cannot travel the road to Heaven, for their bones are broken. "None of the men of strength have found their hands;" in fact, they are "without strength." Happily, it is written, as the commendation of God's love to us:

When we were yet without strength, in due time Christ died for the ungodly (Romans 5:6).

Here we see conscious helplessness succored--succored by the interposition of the Lord Jesus. Our helplessness is extreme. It is not written, "When we were comparatively weak Christ died for us"; or, "When we had only a little strength"; but the description is absolute and unrestricted; "When we were yet without strength." We had no strength whatever which could aid in our salvation; our Lord's words were emphatically true, "Without me ye can do nothing." I may go further than the text, and remind you of the great love wherewith the Lord loved us, "even when we were dead in trespasses and sins." To be dead is even more than to be without strength.

The one thing that the poor strengthless sinner has to fix his mind upon, and firmly retain, as his one ground of hope, is the divine assurance that "in due time Christ died for the ungodly." Believe this, and all inability will disappear. As it is fabled of Midas that he turned everything into gold by his touch, so it is true of faith that it turns everything it touches into good. Our very needs and weaknesses become blessings when faith deals with them.

Let us dwell upon certain forms of this want of strength. To begin with, one man will say, "Sir, I do not seem to have strength to collect my thoughts, and keep them fixed upon those solemn topics which concern my salvation; a short prayer is almost too much for me. It is so partly, perhaps, through natural weakness, partly because I have injured myself through dissipation, and partly also because I worry myself with wordly cares, so that I am not capable of those high thoughts which are necessary ere a soul can be saved." This is a very common form of sinful weakness. Note this! You are without strength on this point; and there are many like you. They could not carry out a train of consecutive thought to save their lives. Many poor men and women are illiterate and untrained, and these would find deep thought to be very heavy work. Others are so light and trifling by nature, that they could no more follow out a long process of argument and reasoning, than they could fly. They could never attain to the knowledge of any profound mystery if they expended their whole life in the effort. *You* need not, therefore, despair: that which is necessary to salvation is not continuous thought, but a simple reliance upon Jesus. Hold you on to this one fact--"In due time Christ died for the ungodly." This truth will not require from you any deep research or profound reasoning, or convincing argument. There it stands: "In due time Christ died for the ungodly." Fix your mind on that, and rest there.

Let this one great, gracious, glorious fact lie in your spirit till it perfumes all your thoughts, and makes you rejoice even though you are without strength, seeing the Lord Jesus has become your strength and your song, yea, He has become your salvation. According to the Scriptures it is a revealed fact, that in due time Christ died for the ungodly when they were yet without strength. You have heard these words hundreds of times, maybe, and yet you have never before perceived their meaning. There is a cheering savor about them, is there not? Jesus did not die for our righteousness, but He died for our sins. He did not come to save us because we were worth the saving, but because we were utterly worthless, ruined, and undone. He came not to earth out of any reason that was in us, but solely and only out of reasons which He fetched from the depths of His own divine love. In due time He died for those whom He describes, not as godly, but as *ungodly*, applying to them as hopeless an adjective as He could well have selected. If you have but little mind, yet fasten it to this truth, which is fitted to the smallest capacity, and is able to cheer the heaviest heart. Let this text lie under your tongue like a sweet morsel, till it dissolves into your heart and flavors all your thoughts; and then it will little matter though those thoughts should be as scattered as autumn leaves. Persons who have never shone in science, nor displayed the least originality of mind, have nevertheless been fully able to accept the doctrine of the cross, and have been saved thereby. *Why should not you?*

I hear another man cry, "*Oh, sir my want of strength lies mainly in this, that I cannot repent sufficiently!*" A curious idea men have of what repentance is! Many fancy that so many tears are to be shed, and so many groans are to be heaved, and so much despair is to be endured. Whence comes this unreasonable notion? Unbelief and despair are sins, and therefore I do not see how they can be constituent elements of acceptable repentance; yet there are many who regard them as necessary parts of true Christian experience. They are in great error. Still, I know what they mean, for in the days of my darkness I used to feel in the same way. I desired to repent, but I thought that I could not do it, and yet all the while I was repenting. Odd as it may sound, I felt that I could not feel. I used to get into a corner and weep, because I could not weep; and I fell into bitter sorrow because I could not sorrow for sin. What a jumble it all is when in our unbelieving state we begin to judge our own condition! It is like a blind man looking at his own eyes. My heart was melted within me for fear, because I thought that my heart was as hard as an adamant stone. My heart was broken to think that it would not break. *Now* I can see that I was exhibiting the very thing which I thought I did not possess; but *then* I knew not where I was.

Oh that I could help others into the light which I now enjoy! Fain would I say a word which might shorten the time of their bewilderment. I would say a few plain words, and pray "the Comforter" to apply them to the heart.

Remember that the man who truly repents is never satisfied with his own repentance. We can no more repent perfectly than we can live perfectly. However pure our tears, there will always be some dirt in them: there will be something to be repented of even in our best repentance. But listen! To repent is to change your mind about sin, and Christ, and all the great things of God. There is sorrow implied in this; but the main point is the turning of the heart from sin to Christ. If there be this turning, you have the essence of true repentance, even though no alarm and no despair should ever have cast their shadow upon your mind.

If you cannot repent as you would, it will greatly aid you to do so if you will firmly believe that "in due time Christ died for the ungodly." Think of this again and again. How can you continue to be hard-hearted when you know that out of supreme love "Christ died for the ungodly"? Let me persuade you to reason with yourself thus: Ungodly as I am, though this heart of steel will not relent, though I smite in vain upon my breast, yet He died for such as I am, since He died for the ungodly. Oh that I may believe this and feel the power of it upon my flinty heart!

Blot out every other reflection from your soul, and sit down by the hour together, and meditate deeply on this one resplendent display of unmerited, unexpected, unexampled love, "Christ died for the ungodly." Read over carefully the narrative of the Lord's death, as you find it in the four evangelists. If anything can melt your stubborn heart, it will be a sight of the sufferings of Jesus, and the consideration that he suffered all this for His enemies.

O Jesus! sweet the tears I shed,
    While at Thy feet I kneel,
Gaze on Thy wounded, fainting head,
    And all Thy sorrows feel.
My heart dissolves to see Thee bleed,
    This heart so hard before;
I hear Thee for the guilty plead,
    And grief o'erflows the more.
'Twas for the sinful Thou didst die,
    And I a sinner stand:
Convinc'd by Thine expiring eye,
    Slain by Thy piercd hand.

Surely the cross is that wonder-working rod which can bring water out of a rock. If you understand the full meaning of the divine sacrifice of Jesus, you must repent of ever having been opposed to One who is so full of love. It is written, "They shall look upon *him* whom they have pierced, and they shall mourn for *him*, as one mourneth for his only son, and shall be in bitterness for him, as one that is in bitterness for his firstborn." Repentance will not make you see Christ; but to see Christ will give you repentance. You may not make a Christ out of your repentance, but you must look for repentance to Christ. The Holy Ghost, by turning us to Christ, turns us from sin. Look away, then, from the effect to the cause, from your own repenting to the Lord Jesus, who is exalted on high to give repentance.

I have heard another say, "*I am tormented with horrible thoughts. Wherever I go, blasphemies steal in upon me. Frequently at my work a dreadful suggestion forces itself upon me, and even on my bed I am startled from my sleep by whispers of the evil one. I cannot get away from this horrible temptation.*" Friend, I know what you mean, for I have myself been hunted by this wolf. A man might as well hope to fight a swarm of flies with a sword as to master his own thoughts when they are set on by the devil. A poor tempted soul, assailed by satanic suggestions, is like a traveler I have read of, about whose head and ears and whole body there came a swarm of angry bees. He could not keep them off nor escape from them. They stung him everywhere and threatened to be the death of him. I do not wonder you feel that you are without strength to stop these hideous and abominable thoughts which Satan pours into your soul; but yet I would remind you of the Scripture before us--"When we were yet without strength, in due time Christ died for the ungodly." Jesus knew where we were and where we should be; He saw that we could not overcome the prince of the power of the air; He knew that we should be greatly worried by him; but even then, when He saw us in that condition, Christ died for the ungodly. Cast the anchor of your faith upon this. The devil himself cannot tell you that you are not ungodly; believe, then, that Jesus died even for such as you are. Remember Martin Luther's way of cutting the devil's head off with his own sword. "Oh," said the devil to Martin Luther, "you are a sinner." "Yes," said he, "Christ died to save sinners." Thus he smote him with his own sword. Hide you in this refuge, and keep there: "In due time Christ died for the ungodly." If you stand to that truth, your blasphemous thoughts which you have not the strength to drive away will go away of themselves; for Satan will see that he is answering no purpose by plaguing you with them.

These thoughts, if you hate them, are none of yours, but are injections of the Devil, for which he is responsible, and not you. If you strive against them, they are no more yours than are the cursings and falsehoods of rioters in the street. It is by means of these thoughts that the Devil would drive you to despair, or at least keep you from trusting Jesus. The poor diseased woman could not come to Jesus for the press, and you are in much the same condition, because of the rush and throng of these dreadful thoughts. Still, she put forth her finger, and touched the fringe of the Lord's garment, and she was healed. Do you the same.

Jesus died for those who are guilty of "all manner of sin and blasphemy," and therefore I am sure He will not refuse those who are unwillingly the captives of evil thoughts. Cast yourself upon Him, thoughts and all, and see if He be not mighty to save. He can still those horrible whisperings of the fiend, or He can enable you to see them in their true light, so that you may not be worried by them. In His own way He can and will save you, and at length give you perfect peace. Only trust Him for this and everything else.

Sadly perplexing is that form of inability which lies in a supposed want of power to believe. We are not strangers to the cry:

Oh that I could believe,

Then all would easy be;

I would, but cannot; Lord, relieve,

My help must come from thee.

Many remain in the dark for years because they have no power, as they say, to do that which is the giving up of all power and reposing in the power of another, even the Lord Jesus. Indeed, it is a very curious thing, this whole matter of believing; for people do not get much help by trying to believe. Believing does not come by trying. If a person were to make a statement of something that happened this day, I should not tell him that I would try to believe him. If I believed in the truthfulness of the man who told the incident to me and said that he saw it, I should accept the statement at once. If I did not think him a true man, I should, of course, disbelieve him; but there would be no *trying* in the matter. Now, when God declares that there is salvation in Christ Jesus, I must either believe Him at once, or make Him a liar. Surely you will not hesitate as to which is the right path in this case, The witness of God must be true, and we are bound at once to believe in Jesus.

But possibly you have been trying to believe too much. Now do not aim at great things. Be satisfied to have a faith that can hold in its hand this one truth, "While we were yet without strength, in due time Christ died for the ungodly." He laid down His life for men while as yet they were not believing in Him, nor were able to believe in Him. He died for men, not as believers, but as sinners. He came to make these sinners into believers and saints; but when He died for them He viewed them as utterly without strength. If you hold to the truth that Christ died for the ungodly, and believe it, your faith will save you, and you may go in peace. If you will trust your soul with Jesus, who died for the ungodly, even though you cannot believe all things, nor move mountains, nor do any other wonderful works, yet you are saved. It is not great faith, but true faith, that saves; and the salvation lies not in the faith, but in the Christ in whom faith trusts. Faith as a grain of mustard seed will bring salvation. It is not the measure of faith, but the sincerity of faith, which is the point to be considered. Surely a man can believe what he knows to be true; and as you know Jesus to be true, you, my friend, can believe in Him.

The cross which is the object of faith, is also, by the power of the Holy Spirit, the cause of it. Sit down and watch the dying Saviour till faith springs up spontaneously in your heart. There is no place like Calvary for creating confidence. The air of that sacred hill brings health to trembling faith. Many a watcher there has said:

While I view Thee, wounded, grieving,
    Breathless on the cursed tree,
Lord, I feel my heart believing
    That Thou suffer'dst thus for me.

"Alas!" cries another, "my want of strength lies in this direction, that I cannot quit my sin, and I know that I cannot go to Heaven and carry my sin with me." I am glad that you know *that*, for it is quite true. You must be divorced from your sin, or you cannot be married to Christ. Recollect the question which flashed into the mind of young Bunyan when at his sports on the green on Sunday: "Wilt thou have thy sins and go to hell, or wilt thou quit thy sins and go to heaven?" That brought him to a dead stand. That is a question which every man will have to answer: for there is no going on in sin and going to heaven. That cannot be. You must quit sin or quit hope. Do you reply, "Yes, I am willing enough. To will is present with me, but how to perform that which l would I find not. Sin masters me, and I have no strength." Come, then, if you have no strength, this text is still true, "When we were yet without strength, in due time Christ died for the ungodly." Can you still believe *that*? However other things may seem to contradict it, will you believe it? God has said it, and it is a fact; therefore, hold on to it like grim death, for your only hope lies there. Believe this and trust Jesus, and you shall soon find power with which to slay your sin; but apart from Him, the strong man armed will hold you for ever his bond slave. Personally, I could never have overcome my own sinfulness. I tried and failed. My evil propensities were too many for me, till, in the belief that Christ died for me, I cast my guilty soul on Him, and then I received a conquering principle by which I overcame my sinful self. The doctrine of the cross can be used to slay sin, even as the old warriors used their huge two-handed swords, and mowed down their foes at every stroke. There is nothing like faith in the sinner's Friend: it overcomes all evil. If Christ has died for me, ungodly as I am, without strength as I am, then I cannot live in sin any longer, but must arouse myself to love and serve Him who hath redeemed me. I cannot trifle with the evil which slew my best Friend. I must be holy for His sake. How can I live in sin when He has died to save me from it?

See what a splendid help this is to you that are without strength, to know and believe that in due time Christ died for such ungodly ones as you are. Have you caught the idea yet? It is, somehow, so difficult for our darkened, prejudiced, and unbelieving minds to see the essence of the gospel. At times I have thought, when I have done preaching, that I have laid down the gospel so clearly, that the nose on one's face could not be more plain; and yet I perceive that even intelligent hearers have failed to understand what was meant by "Look unto me and be ye saved." Converts usually say that they did not know the gospel till such and such a day; and yet they had heard it for years. The gospel is unknown, not from want of explanation, but from absence of personal revelation. This the Holy Ghost is ready to give, and will give to those who ask Him. Yet when given, the sum total of the truth revealed all lies within these words: "Christ died for the ungodly."

I hear another bewailing himself thus: "*Oh, sir, my weakness lies in this, that I do not seem to keep long in one mind! I hear the word on a Sunday, and I am impressed; but in the week I meet with an evil companion, and my good feelings are all gone. My fellow workmen do not believe in anything, and they say such terrible things, and I do not know how to answer them, and so I find myself knocked over.*" I know this Plastic Pliable very well, and I tremble for him; but at the same time, if he is really sincere, his weakness can be met by divine grace. The Holy Spirit can cast out the evil spirit of the fear of man. He can make the coward brave. Remember, my poor vacillating friend, you must not remain in this state. It will never do to be mean and beggarly to yourself. Stand upright, and look at yourself, and see if you were ever meant to be like a toad under a harrow, afraid for your life either to move or to stand still. Do have a mind of your own. This is not a spiritual matter only, but one which concerns ordinary manliness. I would do many things to please my friends; but to go to hell to please them is more than I would venture. It may be very well to do this and that for good fellowship; but it will never do to lose the friendship of God in order to keep on good terms with men. "I know that," says the man, "but still, though I know it, I cannot pluck up courage. I cannot show my colors. I cannot stand fast." Well, to you also I have the same text to bring: "When we were yet without strength, in due time Christ died for the ungodly." If Peter were here, he would say, "The Lord Jesus died for me even when I was such a poor weak creature that the maid who kept the fire drove me to lie, and to swear that I knew not the Lord." Yes, Jesus died for those who forsook him and fled. Take a firm grip on this truth--"Christ died for the ungodly while they were yet without strength." This is your way out of your cowardice. Get this wrought into your soul, "Christ died for me," and you will soon be ready to die for Him. Believe it, that He suffered in your place and stead, and offered for you a full, true, and satisfactory expiation. If you believe that fact, you will be forced to feel, "I cannot be ashamed of Him who died for me." A full conviction that this is true will nerve you with a dauntless courage. Look at the saints in the martyr age. In the early days of Christianity, when this great thought of Christ's exceeding love was sparkling in all its freshness in the church, men were not only ready to die, but they grew ambitious to suffer, and even presented themselves by hundreds at the judgment seats of the rulers, confessing the Christ. I do not say that they were wise to court a cruel death; but it proves my point, that a sense of the love of Jesus lifts the mind above all fear of what man can do to us. Why should it not produce the same effect in you? Oh that it might now inspire you with a brave resolve to come out upon the Lord's side, and be His follower to the end!

May the Holy Spirit help us to come thus far by faith in the Lord Jesus, and it will be well!

THE INCREASE OF FAITH

How can we obtain an increase of faith? This is a very earnest question to many. They say they want to believe, but cannot. A great deal of nonsense is talked upon this subject. Let us be strictly practical in our dealing with it. Common sense is as much needed in religion as anywhere else. "What am I to do in order to believe?" One who was asked the best way to do a certain simple act, replied that the best way to do it was to do it at once. We waste time in discussing methods when the action is simple. The shortest way to believe is to believe. If the Holy Spirit has made you candid, you will believe as soon as truth is set before you. You will believe it because it is true. The gospel command is clear; "Believe in the Lord Jesus Christ, and thou shalt be saved." It is idle to evade this by questions and quibbles. The order is plain; let it be obeyed.

But still, *if you have difficulty, take it before God in prayer*. Tell the great Father exactly what it is that puzzles you, and beg Him by His Holy Spirit to solve the question. If I cannot believe a statement in a book, I am glad to inquire of the author what he means by it; and if he is a true man his explanation will satisfy me; much more will the divine explanation of the hard points of Scripture satisfy the heart of the true seeker. The Lord is willing to make himself known; go to Him and see if it is not so. Repair at once to your closet, and cry, "O Holy Spirit, lead me into the truth! What I know not, teach Thou me."

Furthermore, if faith seems difficult, it is possible that God the Holy Spirit will enable you to believe *if you hear very frequently and earnestly that which you are commanded to believe*. We believe many things because we have heard them so often. Do you not find it so in common life, that if you hear a thing fifty times a day, at last you come to believe it? Some men have come to believe very unlikely statements by this process, and therefore I do not wonder that the good Spirit often blesses the method of often hearing the truth, and uses it to work faith concerning that which is to be believed. It is written, "Faith cometh by hearing"; therefore hear often. If I earnestly and attentively hear the gospel, one of these days I shall find myself believing that which I hear, through the blessed operation of the Spirit of God upon my mind. Only mind you hear *the gospel*, and do not distract your mind with either hearing or reading that which is designed to stagger you.

If that, however, should seem poor advice, I would add next, *consider the testimony of others*. The Samaritans believed because of what the woman told them concerning Jesus. Many of our beliefs arise out of the testimony of others. I believe that there is such a country as Japan; I never saw it, and yet I believe that there is such a place because others have been there. I believe that I shall die; I have never died, but a great many have done so whom I once knew, and therefore I have a conviction that I shall die also. The testimony of many convinces me of that fact. Listen, then, to those who tell you how they were saved, how they were pardoned, how they were changed in character. If you will look into the matter you will find that somebody just like yourself has been saved. If you have been a thief, you will find that a thief rejoiced to wash away his sin in the fountain of Christ's blood. If unhappily you have been unchaste, you will find that men and women who have fallen in that way have been cleansed and changed. If you are in despair, you have only to get among God's people, and inquire a little, and you will discover that some of the saints have been equally in despair at times and they will be pleased to tell you how the Lord delivered them. As you listen to one after another of those who have tried the word of God, and proved it, the divine Spirit will lead you to believe. Have you not heard of the African who was told by the missionary that water sometimes became so hard that a man could walk on it? He declared that he believed a great many things the missionary had told him; but he would never believe that. When he came to England it came to pass that one frosty day he saw the river frozen, but he would not venture on it. He knew that it was a deep river, and he felt certain that he would be drowned if he ventured upon it. He could not be induced to walk the frozen water till his friend and many others went upon it; then he was persuaded, and trusted himself where others had safely ventured. So, while you see others believe in the Lamb of God, and notice their joy and peace, you will yourself be gently led to believe. The experience of others is one of God's ways of helping us to faith. You have either to believe in Jesus or die; there is no hope for you but in Him.

A better plan is this--*note the authority upon which you are commanded to believe*, and this will greatly help you to faith. The authority is not mine, or you might well reject it. But you are commanded to believe upon the authority of God himself. He bids you believe in Jesus Christ, and you must not refuse to obey your Maker. The foreman of a certain works had often heard the gospel, but he was troubled with the fear that he might not come to Christ. His good master one day sent a card around to the works--"Come to my house immediately after work." The foreman appeared at his master's door, and the master came out, and said somewhat roughly, "What do you want, John, troubling me at this time? Work is done, what right have you here?" "Sir," said he, "I had a card from you saying that I was to come after work." "Do you mean to say that merely because you had a card from me you are to come up to my house and call me out after business hours?" "Well, Sir," replied the foreman, "I do not understand you, but it seems to me that, as you sent for me, I had a right to come." "Come in, John," said his master, "I have another message that I want to read to you," and he sat down and read these words: "Come unto me, all ye that labor and are heavy laden, and I will give you rest." "Do you think after such a message from Christ that you can be wrong in coming to him?" The poor man saw it all at once, and believed in the Lord Jesus unto eternal life, because he perceived that he had good warrant and authority for believing. So have you, poor soul! You have good authority for coming to Christ, for the Lord himself bids you trust Him.

If that does not breed faith in you, *think over what it is that you have to believe*--that the Lord Jesus Christ suffered in the place and stead of sinners, and is able to save all who trust Him. Why, this is the most blessed fact that ever men were told to believe; the most suitable, the most comforting, the most divine truth that was ever set before mortal minds. I advise you to think much upon it, and search out the grace and love which it contains. Study the four Evangelists, study Paul's epistles, and then see if the message is not such a credible one that you are forced to believe it.

If that does not do, then *think upon the person of Jesus Christ*--think of *who* He is, and *what* He did, and *where* He is, and *what* He is.

How can you doubt *Him*? It is cruelty to distrust the ever truthful Jesus. He has done nothing to deserve distrust; on the contrary, it should be easy to rely upon Him. Why crucify Him anew by unbelief? Is not this crowning Him with thorns again, and spitting upon Him again? What! is He not to be trusted? What worse insult did the soldiers pour upon Him than this? They made Him a martyr; but you make Him a liar-- this is worse by far. Do not ask *how can I believe?* But answer another question--*How can you disbelieve?*

If none of these things avail, then there is something wrong about you altogether, and my last word is, *submit yourself to God!* Prejudice or pride is at the bottom of this unbelief. May the Spirit of God take away your enmity and make you yield. You are a rebel, a proud rebel, and that is why you do not believe your God. Give up your rebellion; throw down your weapons; yield at discretion, surrender to your King. I believe that never did a soul throw up its hands in self-despair, and cry, "Lord, I yield," but what faith became easy to it before long. It is because you still have a quarrel with God, and resolve to have your own will and your own way, that therefore you cannot believe. "How can ye believe," said Christ, "that have honor one of another?" Proud self creates unbelief. Submit, O man. Yield to your God, and then shall you sweetly believe in your Saviour. May the Holy Ghost now work secretly but effectually with you, and bring you at this very moment to believe in the Lord Jesus! Amen.

REGENERATION AND THE HOLY SPIRIT

"Ye must be born again." This word of our Lord Jesus has appeared to flame in the way of many, like the drawn sword of the cherub at the gate of Paradise. They have despaired, because this change is beyond their utmost effort. The new birth is from above, and therefore it is not in the creature's power. Now, it is far from my mind to deny, or ever to conceal, a truth in order to create a false comfort. I freely admit that the new birth is supernatural, and that it cannot be wrought by the sinner's own self. It would be a poor help to my reader if I were wicked enough to try to cheer him by persuading him to reject or forget what is unquestionably true.

But is it not remarkable that the very chapter in which our Lord makes this sweeping declaration also contains the most explicit statement as to salvation by faith? Read the third chapter of John's Gospel and do not dwell alone upon its earlier sentences. It is true that the third verse says:

> *Jesus answered and said unto him, Verily, verily, I say unto thee, Except a man be born again, he cannot see the kingdom of God.*

But, then, the fourteenth and fifteenth verses speak:

> *And as Moses lifted up the serpent in the wilderness, even so must the Son of man be lifted up: that whosoever believeth in him should not perish, but have eternal life.*

The eighteenth verse repeats the same doctrine in the broadest terms:

> *He that believeth on him is not condemned: but he that believeth not is condemned already, because he hath not believed in the name of the only begotten Son of God.*

It is clear to every reader that these two statements must agree, since they came from the same lips, and are recorded on the same inspired page. Why should we make a difficulty where there can be none? If one statement assures us of the necessity to salvation of a something, which only God can give, and if another assures us that the Lord will save us upon our believing in Jesus, then we may safely conclude that the Lord will give to those who believe all that is declared to be necessary to salvation. The Lord does, in fact, produce the new birth in all who believe in Jesus; and their believing is the surest evidence that they are born again.

We trust in Jesus for what we cannot do ourselves: if it were in our own power, what need of looking to Him? It is ours to believe, it is the Lord's to create us anew. He will not believe for us, neither are we to do regenerating work for Him. It is enough for us to obey the gracious command; it is for the Lord to work the new birth in us. He who could go so far as to die on the cross for us, can and will give us all things that are needful for our eternal safety.

"But a saving change of heart is the work of the Holy Spirit." This also is most true, and let it be far from us to question it, or to forget it. But the work of the Holy Spirit is secret and mysterious, and it can only be perceived by its results. There are mysteries about our natural birth into which it would be an unhallowed curiosity to pry: still more is this the case with the sacred operations of the Spirit of God. "The wind bloweth where it listeth, and thou hearest the sound thereof, but canst not tell whence it cometh, or whither it goeth; so is every one that is born of the Spirit." This much, however, we do know--the mysterious work of the Holy Spirit cannot be a reason for refusing to believe in Jesus to whom that same Spirit beareth witness.

If a man were bidden to sow a field, he could not excuse his neglect by saying that it would be useless to sow unless God caused the seed to grow. He would not be justified in neglecting tillage because the secret energy of God alone can create a harvest. No one is hindered in the ordinary pursuits of life by the fact that unless the Lord build the house they labor in vain that build it. It is certain that no man who believes in Jesus will ever find that the Holy Spirit refuses to work in him: in fact, his believing is the proof that the Spirit is already at work in his heart.

God works in providence, but men do not therefore sit still. They could not move without the divine power giving them life and strength, and yet they proceed upon their way without question; the power being bestowed from day to day by Him in whose hand their breath is, and whose are all their ways. So is it in grace. We repent and believe, though we could do neither if the Lord did not enable us. We forsake sin and trust in Jesus, and then we perceive that the Lord has wrought in us to will and to do of His own good pleasure. It is idle to pretend that there is any real difficulty in the matter.

Some truths which it is hard to explain in words are simple enough in actual experience. There is no discrepancy between the truth that the sinner believes, and that his faith is wrought in him by the Holy Spirit. Only folly can lead men to puzzle themselves about plain matters while their souls are in danger. No man would refuse to enter a lifeboat because he did not know the specific gravity of bodies; neither would a starving man decline to eat till he understood the whole process of mutrition. If you, my reader, will not believe till you can understand all mysteries, you will never be saved at all; and if you allow self-invented difficulties to keep you from accepting pardon through your Lord and Saviour, you will perish in a condemnation which will be richly deserved. Do not commit spiritual suicide through a passion for discussing metaphysical subtleties.

"MY REDEEMER LIVETH"

Continually have I spoken to the reader concerning Christ crucified, who is the great hope of the guilty; but it is our wisdom to remember that our Lord has risen from the dead and lives eternally.

You are not asked to trust in a dead Jesus, but in One who, though He died for our sins, has risen again for our justification. You may go to Jesus at once as to a living and present friend. He is not a mere memory, but a continually existent Person who will hear your prayers and answer them. He lives on purpose to carry on the work for which He once laid down His life. He is interceding for sinners at the right hand of the Father, and for this reason He is able to save them to the uttermost who come unto God by Him. Come and try this living Saviour, if you have never done so before.

This living Jesus is also raised to an eminence of glory and power. He does not now sorrow as "a humble man before his foes," nor labor as "the carpenter's son"; but He is exalted far above principalities and power and every name that is named. The Father has given Him all power in Heaven and in earth, and he exercises this high endowment in carrying out His work of grace. Hear what Peter and the other apostles testified concerning Him before the high priest and the council:

> *The God of our fathers raised up Jesus, whom ye slew and hanged on a tree. Him hath God exalted with his right hand to be a Prince and a Saviour, for to give repentance to Israel, and forgiveness of sins (Acts 5:30, 31).*

The glory which surrounds the ascended Lord should breathe hope into every believer's breast. Jesus is no mean person--He is "a Saviour and a great one." He is the crowned and enthroned Redeemer of men. The sovereign prerogative of life and death is vested in Him; the Father has put all men under the mediatorial government of the Son, so that He can quicken whom He will. He openeth, and no man shuttett. At

His word the soul which is bound by the cords of sin and condemnation can be unloosed in a moment. He stretches out the silver scepter, and whosoever touches it lives.

It is well for us that as sin lives, and the flesh lives, and the devil lives, so Jesus lives; and it is also well that whatever might these may have to ruin us, Jesus has still greater power to save us.

All His exaltation and ability are on our account. "He is exalted to be," and exalted "to give." He is exalted to be a Prince and a Saviour, that He may give all that is needed to accomplish the salvation of all who come under His rule. Jesus has nothing which He will not use for a sinner's salvation, and He is nothing which He will not display in the aboundings of His grace. He links His princedom with His Saviourship, as if He would not have the one without the other; and He sets forth His exaltation as designed to bring blessings to men, as if this were the flower and crown of His glory. Could anything be more calculated to raise the hopes of seeking sinners who are looking Christward?

Jesus endured great humiliation, and therefore there was room for Him to be exalted. By that humiliation He accomplished and endured all the Father's will, and therefore He was rewarded by being raised to glory. He uses that exaltation on behalf of His people. Let my reader raise his eyes to these hills of glory, whence his help must come. Let him contemplate the high glories of the Prince and Saviour. Is it not most hopeful for men that a Man is now on the throne of the universe? Is it not glorious that the Lord of all is the Saviour of sinners? We have a Friend at court; yea, a Friend on the throne. He will use all His influence for those who entrust their affairs in His hands. Well does one of our poets sing:

He ever lives to intercede
> Before His Father's face;

Give Him, my soul, Thy cause to plead,
> No doubt the Father's grace.

Come, friend, and commit your cause and your case to those once pierced hands, which are now glorified with the signet rings of royal power and honor. No suit ever failed which was left with this great Advocate.

REPENTANCE MUST GO WITH FORGIVENESS

It is clear from the text which we have lately quoted that repentance is bound up with the forgiveness of sins. In Acts 5:31 we read that Jesus is *"exalted to give repentance and forgiveness of sins."* These two blessings come from that sacred hand which once was nailed to the tree, but is now raised to glory. Repentance and forgiveness are riveted together by the eternal purpose of God. What God hath joined together let no man put asunder.

Repentance must go with remission, and you will see that it is so if you think a little upon the matter. *It cannot be that pardon of sin should be given to an impenitent sinner;* this were to confirm him in his evil ways, and to teach him to think little of evil. If the Lord were to say, "You love sin, and live in it, and you are going on from bad to worse, but, all the same, I forgive you," this were to proclaim a horrible license for iniquity. The foundations of social order would be removed, and moral anarchy would follow. I cannot tell what innumerable mischiefs would certainly occur if you could divide repentance and forgiveness, and pass by the sin while the sinner remained as fond of it as ever. In the very nature of things, if we believe in *the holiness of God*, it must be so, that if we continue in our sin, and will not repent of it, we cannot be forgiven, but must reap the consequence of our obstinacy. According to the infinite goodness of God, we are promised that if we will forsake our sins, confessing them, and will, by faith, accept the grace which is provided in Christ Jesus, God is faithful and just to forgive us our sins, and to cleanse us from all unrighteousness. But, so long as God lives, there can be no promise of mercy to those who continue in their evil ways, and refuse to acknowledge their wrongdoing. Surely no rebel can expect the King to pardon his treason while he remains in open revolt. No one can be so foolish as to imagine that the Judge of all the earth will put away our sins if we refuse to put them away ourselves.

Moreover, it must be so for *the completeness of divine mercy*. That mercy which could forgive the sin and yet let the sinner live in it would be scant and superficial mercy. It would be unequal and deformed mercy, lame upon one of its feet, and withered as to one of its hands. Which, think you, is the greater privilege, cleansing from the guilt of sin, or deliverance from the power of sin? I will not attempt to weigh in the scales two mercies so surpassing. Neither of them could have come to us apart from the precious blood of Jesus. But it seems to me that to be delivered from the dominion of sin, to be made holy, to be made like to God, must be reckoned the greater of the two, if a comparison has to be drawn. To be forgiven is an immeasurable favor. We make this one of the first notes of our psalm of praise: "Who forgiveth all thine iniquities." But if we could be forgiven, and then could be permitted to love sin, to riot in iniquity, and to wallow in lust, what would be the use of such a forgiveness? Might it not turn out to be a poisoned sweet, which would most effectually destroy us? To be washed, and yet to lie in the mire; to be pronounced clean, and yet to have the leprosy white on one's brow, would be the veriest mockery of mercy. What is it to bring the man out of his sepulcher if you leave him dead? Why lead him into the light if he is still blind? We thank God, that He who forgives our iniquities also heals our diseases. He who washes us from the stains of the past also uplifts us from the foul ways of the present, and keeps us from failing in the future. We must joyfully accept both repentance and remission; they cannot be separated. The covenant heritage is one and indivisible, and must not be parceled out. To divide the work of grace would be to cut the living child in halves, and those who would permit this have no interest in it.

I will ask you who are seeking the Lord, whether you would be satisfied with one of these mercies alone? Would it content you, my reader, if God would forgive you your sin and then allow you to be as worldly and wicked as before? Oh, no! The quickened spirit is more afraid of sin itself than of the penal results of it. The cry of your heart is not, "Who shall deliver me from punishment?" but, "O wretched man that I am! Who shall deliver me from the body of this death? Who shall enable me to live above temptation, and to become holy, even as God is holy?" Since the unity of repentance with remission agrees with gracious desire, and since it is necessary for the completeness of salvation, and for holiness' sake, rest you sure that it abides.

Repentance and forgiveness are joined together *in the experience of all believers.* There never was a person yet who did unfeignedly repent of sin with believing repentance who was not forgiven; and on the other hand, there never was a person forgiven who had not repented of his sin. I do not hesitate to say that beneath the copes of Heaven there never was, there is not, and there never will be, any case of sin being washed away, unless at the same time the heart was led to repentance and faith in Christ. Hatred of sin and a sense of pardon come together into the soul, and abide together while we live.

These two things act and react upon each other: the man who is forgiven, therefore repents; and the man who repents is also most assuredly forgiven. Remember first, that forgiveness leads to repentance. As we sing in Hart's words:

Law and terrors do but harden,

All the while they work alone;

But a sense of blood-bought pardon

Soon dissolves a heart of stone.

When we are sure that we are forgiven, then we abhor iniquity; and I suppose that when faith grows into full assurance, so that we are certain beyond a doubt that the blood of Jesus has washed us whiter than snow, it is then that repentance reaches to its greatest height. Repentance grows as faith grows. Do not make any mistake about it; repentance is not a thing of days and weeks, a temporary penance to be over as fast as possible! No; it is the grace of a lifetime, like faith itself. God's little children repent, and so do the young men and the fathers. Repentance is the inseparable companion of faith. All the while that we walk by faith and not by sight, the tear of repentance glitters in the eye of faith. That is not true repentance which does not come of faith in Jesus, and that is not true faith in Jesus which is not tinctured with repentance. Faith and repentance, like Siamese twins, are vitally joined together. In proportion as we believe in the forgiving love of Christ, in that proportion we repent; and in proportion as we repent of sin and hate evil, we rejoice in the fullness of the absolution which Jesus is exalted to bestow. You will never value pardon unless you feel repentance; and you will never taste the deepest draught of repentance until you know that you are pardoned. It may seem a strange thing, but so it is--the bitterness of repentance and the sweetness of pardon blend in the flavor of every gracious life, and make up an incomparable happiness.

These two covenant gifts are the mutual assurance of each other. If I know that I repent, I know that I am forgiven. How am I to know that I am forgiven except I know also that I am turned from my former sinful course? To be a believer is to be a penitent. Faith and repentance are but two spokes in the same wheel, two handles of the same plough. Repentance has been well described as a heart broken *for* sin, and *from* sin; and it may equally well be spoken of as turning and returning. It is a change of mind of the most thorough and radical sort, and it is attended with sorrow for the past, and a resolve of amendment in the future.

> Repentance is to leave
>> The sins we loved before;
> And show that we in earnest grieve,
>> By doing so no more.

Now, when that is the case, we may be certain that we are forgiven; for the Lord never made a heart to be broken for sin and broken from sin, without pardoning it. If, on the other hand, we are enjoying pardon, through the blood of Jesus, and are justified by faith, and have peace with God, through Jesus Christ our Lord, we know that our repentance and faith are of the right sort.

Do not regard your repentance as the cause of your remission, but as the companion of it. Do not expect to be able to repent until you see the grace of our Lord Jesus, and His readiness to blot out your sin. Keep these blessed things in their places, and view them in their relation to each other. They are the Jachin and Boaz of a saving experience; I mean that they are comparable to Solomon's two great pillars which stood in the forefront of the house of the Lord, and formed a majestic entrance to the holy place. No man comes to God aright except he passes between the pillars of repentance and remission. Upon your heart the rainbow of covenant grace has been displayed in all its beauty when the tear-drops of repentance have been shone upon by the light of full forgiveness. Repentance of sin and faith in divine pardon are the warp and woof of the fabric of real conversion. By these tokens shall you know an Israelite indeed.

To come back to the Scripture upon which we are meditating: both forgiveness and repentance flow from the same source, and are given by the same Saviour. The Lord Jesus in His glory bestows both upon the same persons. You are neither to find the remission nor the repentance elsewhere. Jesus has both ready, and He is prepared to bestow them now, and to bestow them most freely on all who will accept them at His hands. Let it never be forgotten that Jesus gives all that is needful for our salvation. It is highly important that all seekers after mercy should remember this. Faith is as much the gift of God as is the Saviour upon whom that faith relies. Repentance of sin is as truly the work of grace as the making of an atonement by which sin is blotted out. Salvation, from first to last, is of grace alone. You will not misunderstand me. It is not the Holy Spirit who repents. He has never done anything for which He should repent. If He could repent, it would not meet the case; we must ourselves repent of our own sin, or we are not saved from its power. It is not the Lord Jesus Christ who repents. What should He repent of? We ourselves repent with the full consent of every faculty of our mind. The will, the affections, the emotions, all work together most heartily in the blessed act of repentance for sin; and yet at the back of all that is our personal act, there is a secret holy influence which melts the heart, gives contrition, and produces a complete change. The Spirit of God enlightens us to see what sin is, and thus makes it loathsome in our eyes. The Spirit of God also turns us toward holiness, makes us heartily to appreciate, love, and desire it, and thus gives us the impetus by which we are led onward from stage to stage of sanctification. The Spirit of God works in us to will and to do according to God's good pleasure. To that good Spirit let us submit ourselves at once, that He may lead us to Jesus, who will freely give us the double benediction of repentance and remission, according to the riches of His grace.

"BY GRACE ARE YE SAVED."

HOW REPENTANCE IS GIVEN

To return to the grand text: *"Him hath God exalted with his right hand to be a Prince and a Saviour, for to give repentance to Israel, and forgiveness of sins."* Our Lord Jesus Christ has gone up that grace may come down. His glory is employed to give greater currency to His grace. The Lord has not taken a step upward except with the design of bearing believing sinners upward with Him. He is exalted to give repentance; and this we shall see if we remember a few great truths.

The work which our Lord Jesus has done has made repentance possible, available, and acceptable. The law makes no mention of repentance, but says plainly, "The soul that sinneth, it shall die." If the Lord Jesus had not died and risen again and gone unto the Father, what would your repenting or mine be worth? We might feel remorse with its horrors, but never repentance with its hopes. Repentance, as a natural feeling, is a common duty deserving no great praise: indeed, it is so generally mingled with a selfish fear of punishment, that the kindliest estimate makes but little of it. Had not Jesus interposed and wrought out a wealth of merit, our tears of repentance would have been so much water spilled upon the ground. Jesus is exalted on high, that through the virtue of His intercession repentance may have a place before God. In this respect He gives us repentance, because He puts repentance into a position of acceptance, which otherwise it could never have occupied.

When Jesus was exalted on high, *the Spirit of God was poured out to work in us all needful graces.* The Holy Ghost creates repentance in us by supernaturally renewing our nature, and taking away the heart of stone out of our flesh. Oh, sit not down straining those eyes of yours to fetch out impossible tears! Repentance comes not from unwilling nature, but from free and sovereign grace. Get not to your chamber to smite your breast in order to fetch from a heart of stone feelings which are not there. But go to Calvary and see how Jesus died. Look upward to the hills whence comes your help. The Holy Ghost has come on purpose that He may overshadow men's spirits and breed repentance within them, even as once He brooded over chaos and brought forth order. Breathe your prayer to Him, "Blessed Spirit, dwell with me. Make me tender and lowly of heart, that I may hate sin and unfeignedly repent of it." He will hear your cry and answer you.

Remember, too, that when our Lord Jesus was exalted, He not only gave us repentance by sending forth the Holy Spirit, but *by consecrating all the works of nature and of providence to the great ends of our salvation*, so that any one of them may call us to repentance, whether it crow like Peter's cock, or shake the prison like the jailer's earthquake. From the right hand of God our Lord Jesus rules all things here below, and makes them work together for the salvation of His redeemed. He uses both bitters and sweets, trials and joys, that He may produce in sinners a better mind toward their God. Be thankful for the providence which has made you poor, or sick, or sad; for by all this Jesus works the life of your spirit and turns you to Himself. The Lord's mercy often rides to the door of our hearts on the black horse of affliction. Jesus uses the whole range of our experience to wean us from earth and woo us to Heaven. Christ is exalted to the throne of Heaven and earth in order that, by all the processes of His providence, He may subdue hard hearts unto the gracious softening of repentance.

Besides, He is at work at this hour by all His whispers in the conscience, by His inspired Book, by those of us who speak out of that Book, and by praying friends and earnest hearts. He can send a word to you which shall strike your rocky heart as with the rod of Moses, and cause streams of repentance to flow forth. He can bring to your mind some heart-breaking text out of Holy Scripture which shall conquer you right speedily. He can mysteriously soften you, and cause a holy frame of mind to steal over you when you least look for it. Be sure of this, that He who is gone into His glory, raised into all the splendor and majesty of God, has abundant ways of working repentance in those to whom He grants forgiveness. *He is even now waiting to give repentance to you.* Ask Him for it at once.

Observe with much comfort that the *Lord Jesus Christ gives this repentance to the most unlikely people in the world.* He is exalted to give repentance to *Israel*. To Israel! In the days when the apostles thus spoke,

Israel was the nation which had most grossly sinned against light and love, by daring to say, "His blood be on us and on our children." Yet Jesus is exalted to give *them* repentance! What a marvel of grace! If you have been brought up in the brightest of Christian light, and yet have rejected it, there is still hope. If you have sinned against conscience, and against the Holy Spirit, and against the love of Jesus, there is yet space for repentance. Though you may be as hard as unbelieving Israel of old, softening may yet come to you, since Jesus is exalted, and clothed with boundless power. For those who went the furthest in iniquity, and sinned with special aggravation, the Lord Jesus is exalted to give to them repentance and forgiveness of sins. Happy am I to have so full a gospel to proclaim! Happy are you to be allowed to read it!

The hearts of the children of Israel had grown hard as an adamant stone. Luther used to think it impossible to convert a Jew. We are far from agreeing with him, and yet we must admit that the seed of Israel have been exceedingly obstinate in their rejection of the Saviour during these many centuries. Truly did the Lord say, "Israel would none of me." "He came to his own and his own received him not." Yet on behalf of Israel our Lord Jesus is exalted for the giving of repentance and remission. Probably my reader is a Gentile; but yet he may have a very stubborn heart, which has stood out against the Lord Jesus for many years; and yet in him our Lord can work repentance. It may be that you will yet feel compelled to write as William Hone did when he yielded to divine love. He was the author of those most entertaining volumes called the "Everyday Book," but he was once a stout-hearted infidel. When subdued by sovereign grace, he wrote:

> The proudest heart that ever beat
> > Hath been subdued in me;
> The wildest will that ever rose
> To scorn Thy cause and aid Thy foes
> > Is quell'd my Lord, by Thee.
> Thy will, and not my will be done,
> > My heart be ever Thine;
> Confessing Thee the mighty Word,
> My Saviour Christ, my God, my Lord,

Thy cross shall be my sign.

The Lord can give repentance to the most unlikely, turning lions into lambs, and ravens into doves. Let us look to Him that this great change may be wrought in us. Assuredly the contemplation of the death of Christ is one of the surest and speediest methods of gaining repentance. Do not sit down and try to pump up repentance from the dry well of corrupt nature. It is contrary to the laws of mind to suppose that you can force your soul into that gracious state. Take your heart in prayer to Him who understands it, and say, "Lord, cleanse it. Lord, renew it. Lord, work repentance in it." The more you try to produce penitent emotions in yourself, the more you will be disappointed; but if you believingly think of Jesus dying for you, repentance will burst forth. Meditate on the Lord's shedding His heart's blood out of love to you. Set before your mind's eye the agony and bloody sweat, the cross and passion; and, as you do this, He who was the bearer of all this grief will look at you, and with that look He will do for you what He did for Peter, so that you also will go out and weep bitterly. He who died for you can, by His gracious Spirit, make you die to sin; and He who has gone into glory on your behalf can draw your soul after Him, away from evil, and toward holiness.

I shall be content if I leave this one thought with you; look not beneath the ice to find fire, neither hope in your own natural heart to find repentance. Look to the Living One for life. Look to Jesus for all you need between Hell Gate and Heaven Gate. Never seek elsewhere for any part of that which Jesus loves to bestow; but remember,

CHRIST IS ALL.

THE FEAR OF FINAL FALLING

A dark fear haunts the minds of many who are coming to Christ; they are *afraid that they shall not persevere to the end*. I have heard the seeker say: "If I were to cast my soul upon Jesus, yet peradventure I should after all draw back into perdition. I have had good feelings before now, and they have died away. My goodness has been as the morning cloud, and as the early dew. It has come on a sudden, lasted for a season, promised much, and then vanished away."

I believe that this fear is often the father of the fact; and that some who have been afraid to trust Christ for all time, and for all eternity, have failed because they had a temporary faith, which never went far enough to save them. They set out trusting to Jesus in a measure, but looking to themselves for continuance and perseverance in the heavenward way; and so they set out faultily, and, as a natural consequence, turned back before long. If we trust to ourselves for our holding on we shall *not* hold on. Even though we rest in Jesus for a part of our salvation, we shall fail if we trust to self for anything. No chain is stronger than its weakest link: if Jesus be our hope for everything, except one thing, we shall utterly fail, because in that one point we shall come to nought. I have no doubt whatever that a mistake about the perseverance of the saints has prevented the perseverance of many who did run well. What did hinder them that they should not continue to run? They trusted to themselves for that running, and so they stopped short. Beware of mixing even a little of self with the mortar with which you build, or you will make it untempered mortar, and the stones will not hold together. If you look to Christ for your beginnings, beware of looking to yourself for your endings. He is Alpha. See to it that you make Him Omega also. If you begin in the Spirit you must not hope to be made perfect by the flesh. Begin as you mean to go on, and go on as you began, and let the Lord be all in all to you. Oh, that God, the Holy Spirit, may give us a very clear idea of where the strength must come from by which we shall be preserved until the day of our Lord's appearing!

Here is what Paul once said upon this subject when he was writing to the Corinthians:

> *Our Lord Jesus Christ, who shall also confirm you unto the end, that ye may be blameless in the day of our Lord Jesus Christ. God is faithful, by whom ye were called unto the fellowship of his Son Jesus Christ our Lord (1 Cor. 1:8, 9).*

This language silently admits a great need, by telling us how it is provided for. Wherever the Lord makes a provision, we are quite sure that there was a need for it, since no superfluities encumber the covenant of grace. Golden shields hung in Solomon's courts which were never used, but there are none such in the armory of God. What God has provided we shall surely need. Between this hour and the consummation of all things every promise of God and every provision of the covenant of grace will be brought into requisition. The urgent need of the believing soul is confirmation, continuance, final perseverance, preservation to the end. *This is the great necessity of the most advanced believers,* for Paul was writing to saints at Corinth, who were men of a high order, of whom he could say, "I thank my God always on your behalf, for the grace of God which is given you by Jesus Christ." Such men are the very persons who most assuredly feel that they have daily need of new grace if they are to hold on, and hold out, and come off conquerors at the last. If you were not saints you would have no grace, and you would feel no need of more grace; but because you are men of God, therefore you feel the daily demands of the spiritual life. The marble statue requires no food; but the living man hungers and thirsts, and he rejoices that his bread and his water are made sure to him, for else he would certainly faint by the way. The believer's personal wants make it inevitable that he should daily draw from the great source of all supplies; for what could he do if he could not resort to his God?

This is true of the most gifted of the saints--of those men at Corinth who were enriched with all utterance and with all knowledge. They needed to be confirmed to the end, or else their gifts and attainments would prove their ruin. If we had the tongues of men and of angels, if we did not receive fresh grace, where should we be? If we had all experience till we were fathers in the church--if we had been taught of

God so as to understand all mysteries--yet we could not live a single day without the divine life flowing into us from our Covenant Head. How could we hope to hold on for a single hour, to say nothing of a lifetime, unless the Lord should hold us on? He who began the good work in us must perform it unto the day of Christ, or it will prove a painful failure.

This great necessity arises very much from our own selves. In some there is a painful fear that they shall not persevere in grace because they know their own fickleness. Certain persons are constitutionally unstable. Some men are by nature conservative, not to say obstinate; but others are as naturally variable and volatile. Like butterflies they flit from flower to flower, till they visit all the beauties of the garden, and settle upon none of them. They are never long enough in one place to do any good; not even in their business nor in their intellectual pursuits. Such persons may well be afraid that ten, twenty, thirty, forty, perhaps fifty years of continuous religious watchfulness will be a great deal too much for them. We see men joining first one church and then another, till they box the compass. They are everything by turns and nothing long. Such have double need to pray that they may be divinely confirmed, and may be made not only steadfast but unmoveable, or otherwise they will not be found "always abounding in the work of the Lord."

All of us, even if we have no constitutional temptation to fickleness, must feel our own weakness if we are really quickened of God. Dear reader, do you not find enough in any one single day to make you stumble? You that desire to walk in perfect holiness, as I trust you do; you that have set before you a high standard of what a Christian should be--do you not find that before the breakfast things are cleared away from the table, you have displayed enough folly to make you ashamed of yourselves? If we were to shut ourselves up in the lone cell of a hermit, temptation would follow us; for as long as we cannot escape from ourselves we cannot escape from incitements to sin. There is that within our hearts which should make us watchful and humble before God. If he does not confirm us, we are so weak that we shall stumble and fall; not overturned by an enemy, but by our own carelessness. Lord, be thou our strength. We are weakness itself.

Besides that, there is the *weariness which comes of a long life*. When we begin our Christian profession we mount up with wings as eagles, further on we run without weariness; but in our best and truest days we walk without fainting. Our pace seems slower, but it is more serviceable and better sustained. I pray God that the energy of our youth may continue with us so far as it is the energy of the Spirit and not the mere fermentation of proud flesh. He that has long been on the road to Heaven finds that there was good reason why it was promised that his shoes should be iron and brass, for the road is rough. He has discovered that there are Hills of Difficulty and Valleys of Humiliation; that there is a Vale of Deathshade, and, worse still, a Vanity Fair--and all these are to be traversed. If there be Delectable Mountains (and, thank God, there are,) there are also Castles of Despair, the inside of which pilgrims have too often seen. Considering all things, those who hold out to the end in the way of holiness will be "men wondered at."

"O world of wonders, I can say no less." The days of a Christian's life are like so many Koh-i-noors of mercy threaded upon the golden string of divine faithfulness. In Heaven we shall tell to angels, and principalities, and powers, the unsearchable riches of Christ which were spent upon us, and enjoyed by us while we were here below. We have been kept alive on the brink of death. Our spiritual life has been a flame burning on in the midst of the sea, a stone that has remained suspended in the air. It will amaze the universe to see us enter the pearly gate, blameless in the day of our Lord Jesus Christ. We ought to be full of grateful wonder if kept for an hour; and I trust we are.

If this were all, there would be enough cause for anxiety; but there is far more. *We have to think of what a place we live in*. The world is a howling wilderness to many of God's people. Some of us are greatly indulged in the providence of God, but others have a stern fight of it. *We begin our day with prayer, and we hear the voice of holy song full often in our houses*; but many good people have scarcely risen from their knees in the morning before they are saluted with blasphemy. They go out to work, and all day long they are vexed with filthy conversation like righteous Lot in Sodom. Can you even walk the open streets without your ears being afflicted with foul language? The world is no friend to grace. The best we can do with this world is to get through it as quickly as we can, for we dwell in an enemy's country. A robber lurks in every bush. Everywhere we need to travel with a "drawn sword" in our hand, or at least with that weapon which is called *all-prayer* ever at our side; for we have to contend for every inch of our way. Make no mistake about this, or you will be rudely shaken out of your fond delusion. O God, help us, and confirm us to the end, or where shall we be?

True religion is supernatural at its beginning, supernatural in its continuance, and supernatural in its close. It is the work of God from first to last. There is great need that the hand of the Lord should be stretched out still: that need my reader is feeling now, and I am glad that he should feel it; for now he will look for his own preservation to the Lord who alone is able to keep us from failing, and glorify us with His Son.

CONFIRMATION

I want you to notice the security which Paul confidently expected for all the saints. He says--"*Who shall confirm you unto the end, that ye may be blameless in the day of our Lord Jesus Christ.*" This is the kind of confirmation which is above all things to be desired. You see it supposes that the persons are right, and it proposes to confirm them in the right. It would be an awful thing to confirm a man in ways of sin and error. Think of a confirmed drunkard, or a confirmed thief, or a confirmed liar. It would be a deplorable thing for a man to be confirmed in unbelief and ungodliness. Divine confirmation can only be enjoyed by those to whom the grace of God has been already manifested. It is the work of the Holy Ghost. He who gives faith strengthens and establishes it: He who kindles love in us preserves it and increases its flame. What He makes us to know by His first teaching, the good Spirit causes us to know with greater clearness and certainty by still further instruction. Holy acts are confirmed till they become habits, and holy feelings are confirmed till they become abiding conditions. Experience and practice confirm our beliefs and our resolutions. Both our joys and our sorrows, our successes and our failures, are sanctified to the selfsame end: even as the tree is helped to root itself both by the soft showers and the rough winds. The mind is instructed, and in its growing knowledge it gathers reasons for persevering in the good way: the heart is comforted, and so it is made to cling more closely to the consoling truth. The grip grows tighter, and the tread grows firmer, and the man himself becomes more solid and substantial.

This is not a merely natural growth, but is as distinct a work of the Spirit as conversion. *The Lord will surely give it to those who are relying upon Him for eternal life.* By His inward working He will deliver us from being "unstable as water," and cause us to be rooted and grounded. It is a part of the method by which He saves us--this building us up into Christ Jesus and causing us to abide in Him. Dear reader, you may daily look for this; and you shall not be disappointed. He whom you trust will make you to be as a tree planted by the rivers of waters, so preserved that even your leaf shall not wither.

What a strength to a church is a confirmed Christian! He is a comfort to the sorrowful, and a help to the weak. Would you not like to be such? Confirmed believers are pillars in the house of our God. These are not carried away by every wind of doctrine, nor overthrown by sudden temptation. They are a great stay to others, and act as anchors in the time of church trouble. You who are beginning the holy life hardly dare to hope that you will become like them. But you need not fear; the good Lord will work in you as well as in them. One of these days you who are now a "babe" in Christ shall be a "father" in the church. Hope for this great thing; but hope for it as a gift of grace, and not as the wages of work, or as the product of your own energy.

The inspired apostle Paul speaks of these people as to be confirmed *unto the end*. He expected the grace of God to preserve them personally to the end of their lives, or till the Lord Jesus should come. Indeed, he expected that the whole church of God in every place and in all time would be kept to the end of the dispensation, till the Lord Jesus as the Bridegroom should come to celebrate the wedding-feast with his perfected Bride. All who are in Christ will be confirmed in Him till that illustrious day. Has He not said, "Because I live ye shall live also"? He also said, "I give unto my sheep eternal life; and they shall never perish, neither shall any man pluck them out of my hand." He that hath begun a good work in you will confirm it unto the day of Christ. The work of grace in the soul is not a superficial reformation; the life implanted as the new birth comes of a living and incorruptible seed, which liveth and abideth for ever; and the promises of God made to believers are not of a transient character, but involve for their fulfilment the believer's holding on his way till he comes to endless glory. We are kept by the power of God, through faith unto salvation. "The righteous shall hold on his way." Not as the result of our own merit or strength, but as a gift of free and undeserved favor those who believe are "preserved in Christ Jesus." Of the sheep of His fold Jesus will lose none; no member of His Body shall die; no gem of His treasure shall be missing in the day when He makes up His jewels. Dear reader, the salvation which is received by faith is not a thing of months and years;

for our Lord Jesus hath "obtained *eternal* salvation for us," and that which is eternal cannot come to an end.

Paul also declares his expectation that the Corinthian saints would be "Confirmed to the end *blameless*." This blamelessness is a precious part of our keeping. To be kept holy is better than merely to be kept safe. It is a dreadful thing when you see religious people blundering out of one dishonor into another; they have not believed in the power of our Lord to make them blameless. The lives of some professing Christians are a series of stumbles; they are never quite down, and yet they are seldom on their feet. This is not a fit thing for a believer; he is invited to walk with God, and *by faith he can attain to steady perseverance in holiness; and he ought to do so.* The Lord is able, not only to save us from hell, but to keep us from falling. We need not yield to temptation. Is it not written, "Sin shall not have dominion over you?" The Lord is able to keep the feet of His saints; and He will do it if we will trust Him to do so. We need not defile our garments, we may by His grace keep them unspotted from the world; we are bound to do this, "for without holiness no man shall see the Lord."

The apostle prophesied for these believers, that which he would have us seek after--that we may be preserved, *blameless unto the day of our Lord Jesus Christ*." The revised version has "*unreproveable*," instead of "blameless." Possibly a better rendering would be "unimpeachable." God grant that in that last great day we may stand free from all charge, that none in the whole universe may dare to challenge our claim to be the redeemed of the Lord. We have sins and infirmities to mourn over, but these are not the kind of faults which would prove us to be out of Christ; we shall be clear of hypocrisy, deceit, hatred, and delight in sin; for these things would be fatal charges. Despite our failings, the Holy Spirit can work in us a character spotless before men; so that, like Daniel, we shall furnish no occasion for accusing tongues, except in the matter of our religion. Multitudes of godly men and women have exhibited lives so transparent, so consistent throughout, that none could gainsay them. The Lord will be able to say of many a believer, as he did of Job, when Satan stood before Him, "Hast thou considered my servant, a perfect and an upright man, one that feareth God and escheweth evil?" This is what my reader must look for at the Lord's hands. This is the triumph of the saints--to continue to follow the Lamb whithersoever He goeth, maintaining our integrity as before the living God. May we never turn aside into crooked ways, and give cause to the adversary to blaspheme. Of the true believer it is written, "He keepeth himself, and that wicked one toucheth him not." May it be so written concerning us!

Friend just beginning in the divine life, the Lord can give you an irreproachable character. Even though in your past life you may have gone far into sin, the Lord can altogether deliver you from the power of former habits, and make you an example of virtue. He can not only make you moral, but He can make you abhor every false way and follow after all that is saintly. Do not doubt it. The chief of sinners need not be a whit behind the purest of the saints. Believe for this, and according to your faith shall it be unto you.

Oh, what a joy it will be to be found blameless in the day of judgment! We sing not amiss, when we join in that charming hymn:

> Bold shall I stand in that great day,
>
> For who aught to my charge shall lay;
>
> While through Thy blood absolved I am,
>
> From sin's tremendous curse and shame?

What bliss it will be to enjoy that dauntless courage, when heaven and earth shall flee away from the face of the Judge of all! This bliss shall be the portion of everyone who looks alone to the grace of God in Christ Jesus, and in that sacred might wages continual war with all sin.

WHY SAINTS PERSEVERE

The hope which filled the heart of Paul concerning the Corinthian brethren we have already seen to be full of comfort to those who trembled as to their future. But why was it that he believed that the brethren would be confirmed unto the end?

I want you to notice that he gives his reasons. Here they are:

God is faithful, by whom ye were called unto the fellowship of his Son Jesus Christ (1 Cor. 1:9).

The apostle does not say, "*You* are faithful." Alas! the faithfulness of man is a very unreliable affair; it is mere vanity. He does not say, "You have faithful ministers to lead and guide you, and therefore I trust you will be safe." Oh, no! if we are kept by men we shall be but ill kept. He puts it, "God is faithful." If we are found faithful, it will be because God is faithful. On the faithfulness of our covenant God the whole burden of our salvation must rest. On this glorious attribute of God the matter hinges. We are variable as the wind, frail as a spider's web, weak as water. No dependence can be placed upon our natural qualities, or our spiritual attainments; but God abideth faithful. He is faithful in His love; He knows no variableness, neither shadow of turning. He is faithful to His purpose; He doth not begin a work and then leave it undone. He is faithful to His relationships; as a Father He will not renounce His children, as a friend He will not deny His people, as a Creator He will not forsake the work of His own hands. He is faithful to His promises, and will never allow one of them to fail to a single believer. He is faithful to His covenant, which He has made with us in Christ Jesus, and ratified with the blood of His sacrifice. He is faithful to His Son, and will not allow His precious blood to be spilled in vain. He is faithful to His people to whom He has promised eternal life, and from whom He will not turn away.

This faithfulness of God is the foundation and cornerstone of our hope of final perseverance. The saints shall persevere in holiness, because God perseveres in grace. He perseveres to bless, and therefore believers persevere in being blessed. He continues to keep His people, and therefore they continue to keep His commandments. This is good solid ground to rest upon, and it is delightfully consistent with the title of this little book, "ALL OF GRACE." Thus it is free favor and infinite mercy which ring in the dawn of salvation, and the same sweet bells sound melodiously through the whole day of grace.

You see that the only reasons for hoping that we shall be confirmed to the end, and be found blameless at the last, are found in our God; but in Him these reasons are exceedingly abundant.

They lie first, *in what God has done*. He has gone so far in blessing us that it is not possible for Him to run back. Paul reminds us that He has "called us into the fellowship of his Son Jesus Christ." Has he called us? Then the call cannot be reversed; for, "the gifts and calling of God are without repentance." From the effectual call of His grace the Lord never turns. "Whom he called them he also justified, and whom he justified them he also glorified:" this is the invariable rule of the divine procedure. There is a common call, of which it is said, "Many are called, but few are chosen," but this of which we are now thinking is another kind of call, which betokens special love, and necessitates the possession of that to which we are called. In such a case it is with the called one even as with Abraham's seed, of whom the Lord said, "I have called thee from the ends of the earth, and said unto thee, Thou art my servant; I have chosen thee, and not cast thee away."

In what the Lord has done, we see strong reasons for our preservation and future glory, because the Lord has called us *into the fellowship of His Son Jesus Christ*. It means into partnership with Jesus Christ, and I would have you carefully consider what this means. If you are indeed called by divine grace, you have come into fellowship with the Lord Jesus Christ, so as to be joint-owner with Him in all things. Henceforth you are one with Him in the sight of the Most High. The Lord Jesus bare your sins in His own body on the tree, being made a curse for you; and at the same time He has become your righteousness, so that you are justified in Him. You are Christ's and Christ is yours. As Adam stood for his descendants, so does Jesus stand for all who are in Him.

As husband and wife are one, so is Jesus one with all those who are united to Him by faith; one by a conjugal union which can never be broken. More than this, believers are members of the Body of Christ, and so are one with Him by a loving, living, lasting union. God has called us into this union, this fellowship, this partnership, and by this very fact He has given us the token and pledge of our being confirmed to the end. If we were considered apart from Christ we should be poor perishable units, soon dissolved and borne away to destruction; but as one with Jesus we are made partakers of His nature, and are endowed with His immortal life. Our destiny is linked with that of our Lord, and until *He* can be destroyed it is not possible that we should perish.

Dwell much upon this partnership with the Son of God, unto which you have been called: for all your hope lies there. You can never be poor while Jesus is rich, since you are in one firm with Him. Want can never assail you, since you are joint-proprietor with Him who is Possessor of Heaven and earth. You can never fail; for though one of the partners in the firm is as poor as a church mouse, and in himself an utter bankrupt, who could not pay even a small amount of his heavy debts, yet the other partner is inconceivably, inexhaustibly rich. In such partnership you are raised above the depression of the times, the changes of the future, and the shock of the end of all things. The Lord has called you into the fellowship of His Son Jesus Christ, and by that act and deed He has put you into the place of infallible safeguard.

If you are indeed a believer you are one with Jesus, and therefore you are secure. Do you not see that it must be so? You must be confirmed to the end until the day of His appearing, if you have indeed been made one with Jesus by the irrevocable act of God. Christ and the believing sinner are in the same boat: unless Jesus sinks, the believer will never drown. Jesus has taken His redeemed into such connection with himself, that He must first be smitten, overcome, and dishonored, ere the least of His purchased ones can be injured. His name is at the head of the firm, and until it can be dishonored we are secure against all dread of failure.

So, then, with the utmost confidence let us go forward into the unknown future, linked eternally with Jesus. If the men of the world should cry, "Who is this that cometh up from the wilderness, leaning upon her Beloved?" we will joyfully confess that we do lean on Jesus, and that we mean to lean on Him more and more. Our faithful God is an everflowing well of delight, and our fellowship with the Son of God is a full river of joy. Knowing these glorious things we cannot be discouraged: nay, rather we cry with the apostle, *"Who shall separate us from the love of God which is in Christ Jesus our Lord?"*

CLOSE

If my reader has not followed me step by step as he has read my pages, I am truly sorry. Book-reading is of small value unless the truths which pass before the mind are grasped, appropriated, and carried out to their practical issues. It is as if one saw plenty of food in a shop and yet remained hungry, for want of personally eating some. It is all in vain, dear reader, that you and I have met, unless you have actually laid hold upon Christ Jesus, my Lord. On my part there was a distinct desire to benefit you, and I have done my best to that end. It pains me that I have not been able to do you good, for I have longed to win that privilege. I was thinking of you when I wrote this page, and I laid down my pen and solemnly bowed my knee in prayer for everyone who should read it. It is my firm conviction that great numbers of readers will get a blessing, even though *you* refuse to be of the number. But why should *you* refuse? If you do not desire the choice blessing which I would have brought to you, at least do me the justice to admit that the blame of your final doom will not lie at my door. *When we two meet before the great white throne you will not be able to charge me with having idly used the attention which you were pleased to give me while you were reading my little book.* God knoweth I wrote each line for your eternal good. I now in spirit take you by the hand. I give you a firm grip. Do you feel my brotherly grasp? The tears are in my eyes as I look at you and say, *Why will you die?* Will you not give your soul a thought? Will you perish through sheer carelessness? Oh, do not so; but weigh these solemn matters, and make sure work for eternity! Do not refuse Jesus, His love, His blood, His salvation. Why should you do so? Can you do it?

I beseech you,
Do not turn away from your Redeemer!

If, on the other hand, my prayers are heard, and you, my reader, have been led to trust the Lord Jesus and receive from Him salvation by grace, then keep you ever to this doctrine, and this way of living. Let Jesus be your all in all, and let free grace be the one line in which you live and move. There is no life like that of one who lives in the favor of God. To receive all as a free gift preserves the mind from self-righteous pride, and from self-accusing despair. It makes the heart grow warm with grateful love, and thus it creates a feeling in the soul which is infinitely more acceptable to God than anything that can possibly come of slavish fear. Those who hope to be saved by trying to do their best know nothing of that glowing fervor, that hallowed warmth, that devout joy in God, which come with salvation freely given according to the grace of God. The slavish spirit of self-salvation is no match for the joyous spirit of adoption. There is more real virtue in the least emotion of faith than in all the tuggings of legal bond-slaves, or all the weary machinery of devotees who would climb to Heaven by rounds of ceremonies. Faith is spiritual, and God who is a spirit delights in it for that reason. Years of prayer-saying, and church-going, or chapel-going, and ceremonies, and performances, may only be an abomination in the sight of Jehovah; but a glance from the eye of true faith is spiritual and it is therefore dear to Him. "The Father seeketh such to worship him." Look you first to the inner man, and to the spiritual, and the rest will then follow in due course.

If you are saved yourself, be on the watch for the souls of others. Your own heart will not prosper unless it is filled with intense concern to bless your fellow men. The life of your soul lies in faith; its health lies in love. He who does not pine to lead others to Jesus has never been under the spell of love himself. Get to the work of the Lord--the work of love. Begin at home. Visit next your neighbors. Enlighten the village or the street in which you live. Scatter the word of the Lord wherever your hand can reach.

Reader, meet me in heaven! *Do not go down to hell.* There is no coming back again from that abode of misery. Why do you wish to enter the way of death when Heaven's gate is open before you? Do not refuse the free pardon, the full salvation which Jesus grants to all who trust Him. Do not hesitate and delay. You have had enough of resolving, come to action. Believe in Jesus now, with full and immediate decision. Take with you words and come unto your Lord this day, even this day. Remember, O soul, it may be

NOW OR NEVER

with you. Let it be NOW; it would be horrible that it should be *never*.

Again I charge you,

MEET ME IN HEAVEN.

SINNERS IN THE HANDS OF AN ANGRY GOD

By

JONATHAN EDWARDS

Enfield, Connecticut
July 8, 1741

Their foot shall slide in due time. Deuteronomy 32:35

In this verse is threatened the vengeance of God on the wicked unbelieving Israelites, who were God's visible people, and who lived under the means of grace; but who, notwithstanding all God's wonderful works towards them, remained (as vers 28.) void of counsel, having no understanding in them. Under all the cultivations of heaven, they brought forth bitter and poisonous fruit; as in the two verses next preceding the text. -- The expression I have chosen for my text, **their foot shall slide in due time**, seems to imply the following things, relating to the punishment and destruction to which these wicked Israelites were exposed.

1. That they were always exposed to **destruction**; as one that stands or walks in slippery places is always exposed to fall. This is implied in the manner of their destruction coming upon them, being represented by their foot sliding. The same is expressed, Psalm 73:18. *"Surely thou didst set them in slippery places; thou castedst them down into destruction."*

2. It implies, that they were always exposed to **sudden unexpected** destruction. As he that walks in slippery places is every moment liable to fall, he cannot foresee one moment whether he shall stand or fall the next; and when he does fall, he falls at once without warning: Which is also expressed in Psalm 73:18,19. *"Surely thou didst set them in slippery places; thou castedst them down into destruction: How are they brought into desolation as in a moment!"*

3. Another thing implied is, that they are liable to fall **of themselves**, without being thrown down by the hand of another; as he that stands or walks on slippery ground needs nothing but his own weight to throw him down.

4. That the reason why they are not fallen already and do not fall now is only that God's appointed time is not come. For it is said, that when that due time, or appointed time comes, **their foot shall slide**. Then they shall be left to fall, as they are inclined by their own weight. God will not hold them up in these slippery places any longer, but will let them go; and then, at that very instant, they shall fall into destruction; as he that stands on such slippery declining ground, on the edge of a pit, he cannot stand alone, when he is let go he immediately falls and is lost.

The observation from the words that I would now insist upon is this. -- "There is nothing that keeps wicked men at any one moment out of hell, but the mere pleasure of God." -- By the **mere** pleasure of God, I mean his **sovereign** pleasure, his arbitrary will, restrained by no obligation, hindered by no manner of difficulty, any more than if nothing else but God's mere will had in the least degree, or in any respect whatsoever, any hand in the preservation of wicked men one moment. -- The truth of this observation may appear by the following consideration.

1. There is no want of **power** in God to cast wicked men into hell at any moment. Men's hands cannot be strong when God rises up. The strongest have no power to resist him, nor can any deliver out of his hands. -- He is not only able to cast wicked men into hell, but he can most easily do it. Sometimes an earthly prince meets with a great deal of difficulty to subdue a rebel, who has found means to fortify himself, and has made himself strong by the numbers of his followers. But it is not so with God. There is no fortress that is any defence from the power of God. Though hand join in hand, and vast multitudes of God's enemies combine and associate themselves, they are easily broken in pieces. They are as great heaps of light chaff before the whirlwind; or large quantities of dry stubble before devouring flames. We find it easy to tread on and crush a worm that we see crawling on the earth; so it is easy for us to cut or singe a slender thread that any thing hangs by: thus easy is it for God, when he pleases, to cast his enemies down to hell. What are we, that we should think to stand before him, at whose rebuke the earth trembles, and before whom the rocks are thrown down?

2.   They **deserve** to be cast into hell; so that divine justice never stands in the way, it makes no objection against God's using his power at any moment to destroy them. Yea, on the contrary, justice calls aloud for an infinite punishment of their sins. Divine justice says of the tree that brings forth such grapes of Sodom, "*Cut it down, why cumbereth it the ground?*" Luke 13:7. The sword of divine justice is every moment brandished over their heads, and it is nothing but the hand of arbitrary mercy, and God's mere will, that holds it back.

3.   They are already under a sentence of **condemnation** to hell. They do not only justly deserve to be cast down thither, but the sentence of the law of God, that eternal and immutable rule of righteousness that God has fixed between him and mankind, is gone out against them, and stands against them; so that they are bound over already to hell. John 3:18. "*He that believeth not is condemned already.*" So that every unconverted man properly belongs to hell; that is his place; from thence he is, John 8:23. "*Ye are from beneath:*" And thither he is bound; it is the place that justice, and God's word, and the sentence of his unchangeable law assign to him.

4.   They are now the objects of that very same **anger** and wrath of God, that is expressed in the torments of hell. And the reason why they do not go down to hell at each moment, is not because God, in whose power they are, is not then very angry with them; as he is with many miserable creatures now tormented in hell, who there feel and bear the fierceness of his wrath. Yea, God is a great deal more angry with great numbers that are now on earth: yea, doubtless, with many that are now in this congregation, who it may be are at ease, than he is with many of those who are now in the flames of hell.

So that it is not because God is unmindful of their wickedness, and does not resent it, that he does not let loose his hand and cut them off. God is not altogether such an one as themselves, though they may imagine him to be so. The wrath of God burns against them, their damnation does not slumber; the pit is prepared, the fire is made ready, the furnace is now hot, ready to receive them; the flames do now rage and glow. The glittering sword is whet, and held over them, and the pit hath opened its mouth under them.

5.   The **devil** stands ready to fall upon them, and seize them as his own, at what moment God shall permit him. They belong to him; he

has their souls in his possession, and under his dominion. The scripture represents them as his goods, Luke 11:21. The devils watch them; they are ever by them at their right hand; they stand waiting for them, like greedy hungry lions that see their prey, and expect to have it, but are for the present kept back. If God should withdraw his hand, by which they are restrained, they would in one moment fly upon their poor souls. The old serpent is gaping for them; hell opens its mouth wide to receive them; and if God should permit it, they would be hastily swallowed up and lost.

6. There are in the souls of wicked men those hellish **principles** reigning, that would presently kindle and flame out into hell fire, if it were not for God's restraints. There is laid in the very nature of carnal men, a foundation for the torments of hell. There are those corrupt principles, in reigning power in them, and in full possession of them, that are seeds of hell fire. These principles are active and powerful, exceeding violent in their nature, and if it were not for the restraining hand of God upon them, they would soon break out, they would flame out after the same manner as the same corruptions, the same enmity does in the hearts of damned souls, and would beget the same torments as they do in them. The souls of the wicked are in scripture compared to the troubled sea, Isa. 57:20. For the present, God restrains their wickedness by his mighty power, as he does the raging waves of the troubled sea, saying, "*Hitherto shalt thou come, but no further;*" but if God should withdraw that restraining power, it would soon carry all before it. Sin is the ruin and misery of the soul; it is destructive in its nature; and if God should leave it without restraint, there would need nothing else to make the soul perfectly miserable. The corruption of the heart of man is immoderate and boundless in its fury; and while wicked men live here, it is like fire pent up by God's restraints, whereas if it were let loose, it would set on fire the course of nature; and as the heart is now a sink of sin, so if sin was not restrained, it would immediately turn the soul into fiery oven, or a furnace of fire and brimstone.

7. It is no security to wicked men for one moment, that there are no visible means of death at hand. It is no security to a natural man, that he is now in health, and that he does not see which way he should now immediately go out of the world by any accident, and that there is no visible danger in any respect in his circumstances. The manifold

and continual experience of the world in all ages, shows this is no evidence, that a man is not on the very brink of eternity, and that the next step will not be into another world. The unseen, unthought-of ways and means of persons going suddenly out of the world are innumerable and inconceivable. Unconverted men walk over the pit of hell on a rotten covering, and there are innumerable places in this covering so weak that they will not bear their weight, and these places are not seen. The arrows of death fly unseen at noon-day; the sharpest sight cannot discern them. God has so many different unsearchable ways of taking wicked men out of the world and sending them to hell, that there is nothing to make it appear, that God had need to be at the expense of a miracle, or go out of the ordinary course of his providence, to destroy any wicked man, at any moment. All the means that there are of sinners going out of the world, are so in God's hands, and so universally and absolutely subject to his power and determination, that it does not depend at all the less on the mere will of God, whether sinners shall at any moment go to hell, than if means were never made use of, or at all concerned in the case.

8. Natural men's prudence and care to preserve their own lives, or the care of others to preserve them, do not secure them a moment. To this, divine providence and universal experience do also bear testimony. There is this clear evidence that men's own wisdom is no security to them from death; that if it were otherwise we should see some difference between the wise and politic men of the world, and others, with regard to their liableness to early and unexpected death: but how is it in fact? Eccles. 2:16. *"How dieth the wise man? even as the fool."*

9. All wicked men's pains and **contrivance** which they use to escape hell, while they continue to reject Christ, and so remain wicked men, do not secure them from hell one moment. Almost every natural man that hears of hell, flatters himself that he shall escape it; he depends upon himself for his own security; he flatters himself in what he has done, in what he is now doing, or what he intends to do. Every one lays out matters in his own mind how he shall avoid damnation, and flatters himself that he contrives well for himself, and that his schemes will not fail. They hear indeed that there are but few saved, and that the greater part of men that have died heretofore are gone to hell; but each one imagines that he lays out matters better for his own escape than

others have done. He does not intend to come to that place of torment; he says within himself, that he intends to take effectual care, and to order matters so for himself as not to fail.

But the foolish children of men miserably delude themselves in their own schemes, and in confidence in their own strength and wisdom; they trust to nothing but a shadow. The greater part of those who heretofore have lived under the same means of grace, and are now dead, are undoubtedly gone to hell; and it was not because they were not as wise as those who are now alive: it was not because they did not lay out matters as well for themselves to secure their own escape. If we could speak with them, and inquire of them, one by one, whether they expected, when alive, and when they used to hear about hell, ever to be the subjects of misery: we doubtless, should hear one and another reply, "No, I never intended to come here: I had laid out matters otherwise in my mind; I thought I should contrive well for myself -- I thought my scheme good. I intended to take effectual care; but it came upon me unexpected; I did not look for it at that time, and in that manner; it came as a thief -- Death outwitted me: God's wrath was too quick for me. Oh, my cursed foolishness! I was flattering myself, and pleasing myself with vain dreams of what I would do hereafter; and when I was saying, Peace and safety, then sudden destruction came upon me."

10. God has laid himself under no **obligation**, by any promise to keep any natural man out of hell one moment. God certainly has made no promises either of eternal life, or of any deliverance or preservation from eternal death, but what are contained in the covenant of grace, the promises that are given in Christ, in whom all the promises are yea and amen. But surely they have no interest in the promises of the covenant of grace who are not the children of the covenant, who do not believe in any of the promises, and have no interest in the Mediator of the covenant.

So that, whatever some have imagined and pretended about promises made to natural men's earnest seeking and knocking, it is plain and manifest, that whatever pains a natural man takes in religion, whatever prayers he makes, till he believes in Christ, God is under no manner of obligation to keep him a moment from eternal destruction.

So that, thus it is that natural men are held in the hand of God, over the pit of hell; they have deserved the fiery pit, and are already sentenced to it; and God is dreadfully provoked, his anger is as great towards them as to those that are actually suffering the executions of the fierceness of his wrath in hell, and they have done nothing in the least to appease or abate that anger, neither is God in the least bound by any promise to hold them up one moment; the devil is waiting for them, hell is gaping for them, the flames gather and flash about them, and would fain lay hold on them, and swallow them up; the fire pent up in their own hearts is struggling to break out: and they have no interest in any Mediator, there are no means within reach that can be any security to them. In short, they have no refuge, nothing to take hold of; all that preserves them every moment is the mere arbitrary will, and uncovenanted, unobliged forbearance of an incensed God.

Application

The use of this awful subject may be for awakening unconverted persons in this congregation. This that you have heard is the case of every one of you that are out of Christ. -- That world of misery, that lake of burning brimstone, is extended abroad under you. There is the dreadful pit of the glowing flames of the wrath of God; there is hell's wide gaping mouth open; and you have nothing to stand upon, nor any thing to take hold of; there is nothing between you and hell but the air; it is only the power and mere pleasure of God that holds you up.

You probably are not sensible of this; you find you are kept out of hell, but do not see the hand of God in it; but look at other things, as the good state of your bodily constitution, your care of your own life, and the means you use for your own preservation. But indeed these things are nothing; if God should withdraw his hand, they would avail no more to keep you from falling, than the thin air to hold up a person that is suspended in it.

Your wickedness makes you as it were heavy as lead, and to tend downwards with great weight and pressure towards hell; and if God should let you go, you would immediately sink and swiftly descend and plunge into the bottomless gulf, and your healthy constitution, and your own care and prudence, and best contrivance, and all your righteousness, would have no more influence to uphold you and keep you out of hell, than a spider's web would have to stop a falling rock. Were it not for the sovereign pleasure of God, the earth would not bear you one moment; for you are a burden to it; the creation groans with you; the creature is made subject to the bondage of your corruption, not willingly; the sun does not willingly shine upon you to give you light to serve sin and Satan; the earth does not willingly yield her increase to satisfy your lusts; nor is it willingly a stage for your wickedness to be acted upon; the air does not willingly serve you for breath to maintain the flame of life in your vitals, while you spend your life in the service of God's enemies. God's creatures are good, and were made for men to serve God with, and do not willingly subserve to any other purpose, and groan when they are abused to purposes so directly contrary to their nature and end. And the world would spew you out, were it not for the sovereign hand of him who hath subjected it in hope. There are the black clouds of God's wrath now hanging directly over your heads, full of the dreadful storm, and big with thunder; and were it not for the restraining hand of God, it would immediately burst forth upon you. The sovereign pleasure of God, for the present, stays his rough wind; otherwise it would come with fury, and your destruction would come like a whirlwind, and you would be like the chaff on the summer threshing floor.

The wrath of God is like great waters that are dammed for the present; they increase more and more, and rise higher and higher, till an outlet is given; and the longer the stream is stopped, the more rapid and mighty is its course, when once it is let loose. It is true, that judgment against your evil works has not been executed hitherto; the floods of God's vengeance have been withheld; but your guilt in the mean time is constantly increasing, and you are every day treasuring up more wrath; the waters are constantly rising, and waxing more and more mighty; and there is nothing but the mere pleasure of God, that holds the waters back, that are unwilling to be stopped, and press hard to go forward. If God should only withdraw his hand from the flood-gate, it would immediately fly open, and the fiery floods of the fierceness and wrath of God, would rush forth with inconceivable fury, and would come upon you with omnipotent power; and if your strength were ten thousand times greater than it is, yea, ten thousand times greater than the strength of the stoutest, sturdiest devil in hell, it would be nothing to withstand or endure it.

The bow of God's wrath is bent, and the arrow made ready on the string, and justice bends the arrow at your heart, and strains the bow, and it is nothing but the mere pleasure of God, and that of an angry God, without any promise or obligation at all, that keeps the arrow one moment from being made drunk with your blood. Thus all you that never passed under a great change of heart, by the mighty power of the Spirit of God upon your souls; all you that were never born again, and made new creatures, and raised from being dead in sin, to a state of new, and before altogether unexperienced light and life, are in the hands of an angry God. However you may have reformed your life in many things, and may have had religious affections, and may keep up a form of religion in your families and closets, and in the house of God, it is nothing but his mere pleasure that keeps you from being this moment swallowed up in everlasting destruction. However unconvinced you may now be of the truth of what you hear, by and by you will be fully convinced of it. Those that are gone from being in the like circumstances with you, see that it was so with them; for destruction came suddenly upon most of them; when they expected nothing of it, and while they were saying, Peace and safety: now they see, that those things on which they depended for peace and safety, were nothing but thin air and empty shadows.

The God that holds you over the pit of hell, much as one holds a spider, or some loathsome insect over the fire, abhors you, and is dreadfully provoked: his wrath towards you burns like fire; he looks upon you as worthy of nothing else, but to be cast into the fire; he is of purer eyes than to bear to have you in his sight; you are ten thousand times more abominable in his eyes, than the most hateful venomous serpent is in ours. You have offended him infinitely more than ever a stubborn rebel did his prince; and yet it is nothing but his hand that holds you from falling into the fire every moment. It is to be ascribed to nothing else, that you did not go to hell the last night; that you was suffered to awake again in this world, after you closed your eyes to sleep. And there is no other reason to be given, why you have not dropped into hell since you arose in the morning, but that God's hand has held you up. There is no other reason to be given why you have not gone to hell, since you have sat here in the house of God, provoking his pure eyes by your sinful wicked manner of attending his solemn worship. Yea, there is nothing else that is to be given as a reason why you do not this very moment drop down into hell.

O sinner! Consider the fearful danger you are in: it is a great furnace of wrath, a wide and bottomless pit, full of the fire of wrath, that you are held over in the hand of that God, whose wrath is provoked and incensed as much against you, as against many of the damned in hell. You hang by a slender thread, with the flames of divine wrath flashing about it, and ready every moment to singe it, and burn it asunder;

and you have no interest in any Mediator, and nothing to lay hold of to save yourself, nothing to keep off the flames of wrath, nothing of your own, nothing that you ever have done, nothing that you can do, to induce God to spare you one moment. -- And consider here more particularly,

    1.   **Whose** wrath it is: it is the wrath of the infinite God. If it were only the wrath of man, though it were of the most potent prince, it would be comparatively little to be regarded. The wrath of kings is very much dreaded, especially of absolute monarchs, who have the possessions and lives of their subjects wholly in their power, to be disposed of at their mere will. Prov. 20:2. "*The fear of a king is as the roaring of a lion: Whoso provoketh him to anger, sinneth against his own soul.*" The subject that very much enrages an arbitrary prince, is liable to suffer the most extreme torments that human art can invent, or human power can inflict. But the greatest earthly potentates in their greatest majesty and strength, and when clothed in their greatest terrors, are but feeble, despicable worms of the dust, in comparison of the great and almighty Creator and King of heaven and earth. It is but little that they can do, when most enraged, and when they have exerted the utmost of their fury. All the kings of the earth, before God, are as grasshoppers; they are nothing, and less than nothing: both their love and their hatred is to be despised. The wrath of the great King of kings, is as much more terrible than theirs, as his majesty is greater. Luke 12:4,5. "*And I say unto you, my friends, Be not afraid of them that kill the body, and after that, have no more that they can do. But I will forewarn you whom you shall fear: fear him, which after he hath killed, hath power to cast into hell: yea, I say unto you, Fear him.*"

    2.   It is the **fierceness** of his wrath that you are exposed to. We often read of the fury of God; as in Isa. 59:18. "*According to their deeds, accordingly he will repay fury to his adversaries.*" So Isa. 66:15. "*For behold, the Lord will come with fire, and with his chariots like a whirlwind, to render his anger with fury, and his rebuke with flames of fire.*" And in many other places. So, Rev. 19:15, we read of "*the wine press of the fierceness and wrath of Almighty God.*" The words are exceeding terrible. If it had only been said, "*the wrath of God,*" the words would have implied that which is infinitely dreadful: but it is "*the fierceness and wrath of God.*" The fury of God! the fierceness of Jehovah! Oh, how

dreadful that must be! Who can utter or conceive what such expressions carry in them! But it is also *"the fierceness and wrath of **almighty** God."* As though there would be a very great manifestation of his almighty power in what the fierceness of his wrath should inflict, as though omnipotence should be as it were enraged, and exerted, as men are wont to exert their strength in the fierceness of their wrath. Oh! then, what will be the consequence! What will become of the poor worms that shall suffer it! Whose hands can be strong? And whose heart can endure? To what a dreadful, inexpressible, inconceivable depth of misery must the poor creature be sunk who shall be the subject of this!

Consider this, you that are here present, that yet remain in an unregenerate state. That God will execute the fierceness of his anger, implies, that he will inflict wrath without any pity. When God beholds the ineffable extremity of your case, and sees your torment to be so vastly disproportioned to your strength, and sees how your poor soul is crushed, and sinks down, as it were, into an infinite gloom; he will have no compassion upon you, he will not forbear the executions of his wrath, or in the least lighten his hand; there shall be no moderation or mercy, nor will God then at all stay his rough wind; he will have no regard to your welfare, nor be at all careful lest you should suffer too much in any other sense, than only that you shall **not suffer beyond what strict justice requires**. Nothing shall be withheld, because it is so hard for you to bear. Ezek. 8:18. *"Therefore will I also deal in fury: mine eye shall not spare, neither will I have pity; and though they cry in mine ears with a loud voice, yet I will not hear them."* Now God stands ready to pity you; this is a day of mercy; you may cry now with some encouragement of obtaining mercy. But when once the day of mercy is past, your most lamentable and dolorous cries and shrieks will be in vain; you will be wholly lost and thrown away of God, as to any regard to your welfare. God will have no other use to put you to, but to suffer misery; you shall be continued in being to no other end; for you will be a vessel of wrath fitted to destruction; and there will be no other use of this vessel, but to be filled full of wrath. God will be so far from pitying you when you cry to him, that it is said he will only *"laugh and mock,"* Prov. 1:25,26, etc.

How awful are those words, Isa. 63:3, which are the words of the great God. *"I will tread them in mine anger, and will trample them in my fury, and their blood shall be sprinkled upon my garments, and I will stain all my raiment."* It is perhaps impossible to conceive of words that carry in them greater manifestations of these three things, viz. contempt, and hatred, and fierceness of indignation. If you cry to God to pity you, he will be so far from pitying you in your doleful case, or showing you the least regard or favour, that instead of that, he will only tread you under foot. And though he will know that you cannot bear the weight of omnipotence treading upon you, yet he will not regard that, but he will crush you under his feet without mercy; he will crush out your blood, and make it fly, and it shall be sprinkled on his garments, so as to stain all his raiment. He will not only hate you, but he will have you in the utmost contempt: no place shall be thought fit for you, but under his feet to be trodden down as the mire of the streets.

3. The **misery** you are exposed to is that which God will inflict to that end, that he might show what that wrath of Jehovah is. God hath had it on his heart to show to angels and men, both how excellent his love is, and also how terrible his wrath is. Sometimes earthly kings have a mind to show how terrible their wrath is, by the extreme punishments they would execute on those that would provoke them. Nebuchadnezzar, that mighty and haughty monarch of the Chaldean empire, was willing to show his wrath when enraged with Shadrach, Meshach, and Abednego; and accordingly gave orders that the burning fiery furnace should be heated seven times hotter than it was before; doubtless, it was raised to the utmost degree of fierceness that human art could raise it. But the great God is also willing to show his wrath, and magnify his awful majesty and mighty power in the extreme sufferings of his enemies. Rom. 9:22. *"What if God, willing to show his wrath, and to make his power known, endured with much long-suffering the vessels of wrath fitted to destruction?"* And seeing this is his design, and what he has determined, even to show how terrible the unrestrained wrath, the fury and fierceness of Jehovah is, he will do it to effect. There will be something accomplished and brought to pass that will be dreadful with a witness. When the great and angry God hath risen up and executed his awful vengeance on the poor sinner, and the wretch is actually suffering the infinite weight and power of his indignation, then will God call upon the whole universe to behold that awful majesty and mighty power that is to be seen in it. Isa. 33:12-14. *"And the people shall be as*

the burnings of lime, as thorns cut up shall they be burnt in the fire. Hear ye that are far off, what I have done; and ye that are near, acknowledge my might. The sinners in Zion are afraid; fearfulness hath surprised the hypocrites," etc.

Thus it will be with you that are in an unconverted state, if you continue in it; the infinite might, and majesty, and terribleness of the omnipotent God shall be magnified upon you, in the ineffable strength of your torments. You shall be tormented in the presence of the holy angels, and in the presence of the Lamb; and when you shall be in this state of suffering, the glorious inhabitants of heaven shall go forth and look on the awful spectacle, that they may see what the wrath and fierceness of the Almighty is; and when they have seen it, they will fall down and adore that great power and majesty. Isa. 66:23,24. "*And it shall come to pass, that from one new moon to another, and from one sabbath to another, shall all flesh come to worship before me, saith the Lord. And they shall go forth and look upon the carcasses of the men that have transgressed against me; for their worm shall not die, neither shall their fire be quenched, and they shall be an abhorring unto all flesh.*"

4. It is **everlasting** wrath. It would be dreadful to suffer this fierceness and wrath of Almighty God one moment; but you must suffer it to all eternity. There will be no end to this exquisite horrible misery. When you look forward, you shall see a long for ever, a boundless duration before you, which will swallow up your thoughts, and amaze your soul; and you will absolutely despair of ever having any deliverance, any end, any mitigation, any rest at all. You will know certainly that you must wear out long ages, millions of millions of ages, in wrestling and conflicting with this almighty merciless vengeance; and then when you have so done, when so many ages have actually been spent by you in this manner, you will know that all is but a point to what remains. So that your punishment will indeed be infinite. Oh, who can express what the state of a soul in such circumstances is! All that we can possibly say about it, gives but a very feeble, faint representation of it; it is inexpressible and inconceivable: For "*who knows the power of God's anger?*"

How dreadful is the state of those that are daily and hourly in the danger of this great wrath and infinite misery! But this is the dismal case of every soul in this congregation that has not been born again, however moral and strict, sober and religious, they may otherwise be. Oh that you would consider it, whether you be young or old! There is reason to think, that there are many in this congregation now hearing this discourse, that will actually be the subjects of this very misery to all eternity. We know not who they are, or in what seats they sit, or what thoughts they now have. It may be they are now at ease, and hear all these things without much disturbance, and are now flattering themselves that they are not the persons, promising themselves that they shall escape. If we knew that there was one person, and but one, in the whole congregation, that was to be the subject of this misery, what an awful thing would it be to think of! If we knew who it was, what an awful sight would it be to see such a person! How might all the rest of the congregation lift up a lamentable and bitter cry over him! But, alas! instead of one, how many is it likely will remember this discourse in hell? And it would be a wonder, if some that are now present should not be in hell in a very short time, even before this year is out. And it would be no wonder if some persons, that now sit here, in some seats of this meeting-house, in health, quiet and secure, should be there before tomorrow morning. Those of you that finally continue in a natural condition, that shall keep out of hell longest will be there in a little time! your damnation does not slumber; it will come swiftly, and, in all probability, very suddenly upon many of you. You have reason to wonder that you are not already in hell. It is doubtless the case of some whom you have seen and known, that never deserved hell more than you, and that heretofore appeared as likely to have been now alive as you. Their case is past all hope; they are crying in extreme misery and perfect despair; but here you are in the land of the living and in the house of God, and have an opportunity to obtain salvation. What would not those poor damned hopeless souls give for one day's opportunity such as you now enjoy!

And now you have an extraordinary opportunity, a day wherein Christ has thrown the door of mercy wide open, and stands in calling and crying with a loud voice to poor sinners; a day wherein many are flocking to him, and pressing into the kingdom of God. Many are daily coming from the east, west, north and south; many that were very lately in the same miserable condition that you are in, are now in a happy state, with their hearts filled with love to him who has loved them, and washed them from their sins in his own blood, and rejoicing in hope of the glory of God. How awful is it to be left behind at such a day! To see so many others feasting, while you are pining and perishing! To see so many rejoicing and singing for joy of heart, while you have cause to mourn for sorrow of heart, and howl for vexation of spirit! How can you rest one moment in such a condition? Are not your souls as precious as the souls of the people at Suffield, where they are flocking from day to day to Christ?

Are there not many here who have lived long in the world, and are not to this day born again? and so are aliens from the commonwealth of Israel, and have done nothing ever since they have lived, but treasure up wrath against the day of wrath? Oh, sirs, your case, in an especial manner, is extremely dangerous. Your guilt and hardness of heart is extremely great. Do you not see how generality persons of your years are passed over and left, in the present remarkable and wonderful dispensation of God's mercy? You had need to consider yourselves, and awake thoroughly out of sleep. You cannot bear the fierceness and wrath of the infinite God. -- And you, young men, and young women, will you neglect this precious season which you now enjoy, when so many others of your age are renouncing all youthful vanities, and flocking to Christ? You especially have now an extraordinary opportunity; but if you neglect it, it will soon be with you as with those persons who spent all the precious days of youth in sin, and are now come to such a dreadful pass in blindness and hardness. -- And you, children, who are unconverted, do not you know that you are going down to hell, to bear the dreadful wrath of that God, who is now angry with you every day and every night? Will you be content to be the children of the devil, when so many other children in the land are converted, and are become the holy and happy children of the King of kings?

And let every one that is yet out of Christ, and hanging over the pit of hell, whether they be old men and women, or middle aged, or young people, or little children, now hearken to the loud calls of God's word and providence. This acceptable year of the Lord, a day of such great favour to some, will doubtless be a day of as remarkable vengeance to others. Men's hearts harden, and their guilt increases apace at such a day as this, if they neglect their souls; and never was there so great danger of such persons being given up to hardness of heart and blindness of mind. God seems now to be hastily gathering in his elect in all parts of the land; and probably the greater part of adult persons that ever shall be saved, will be brought in now in a little time, and that it will be as it was on the great out-pouring of the Spirit upon the Jews in the apostles' days; the election will obtain, and the rest will be blinded. If this should be the case with you, you will eternally curse this day, and will curse the day that ever you was born, to see such a season of the pouring out of God's Spirit, and will wish that you had died and gone to hell before you had seen it. Now undoubtedly it is, as it was in the days of John the Baptist, the axe is in an extraordinary manner laid at the root of the trees, that every tree which brings not forth good fruit, may be hewn down and cast into the fire.

Therefore, let every one that is out of Christ, now awake and fly from the wrath to come. The wrath of Almighty God is now undoubtedly hanging over a great part of this congregation. Let every one fly out of Sodom: "Haste and escape for your lives, look not behind you, escape to the mountain, lest you be consumed."

Made in the USA
Coppell, TX
15 July 2021